MISSION

Understanding Your Role in God's "Unfulfilled Assignment"

DAVID LITWIN
Author of *Parables & Parallels*

PURE FUSION MEDIA
FRANKLIN, TENNESSEE

Printed in the United States of America

All rights reserved. No part of this publication may be reproduced, stored in a retrieval system, or transmitted in any form or by any means for example, electronic, photocopy, recording without the prior permission of the publisher. The only exception is brief quotations in printed/online reviews.

Scripture quotations marked NASB are taken from the NEW AMERICAN STANDARD BIBLE®, Copyright © 1960,1962,1963,1968,1971,1972,1973,1975,1977,1995 by The Lockman Foundation. Used by permission.

Scripture quotations marked NKJV are taken from the New King James Version®. Copyright © 1982 by Thomas Nelson, Inc. Used by permission. All rights reserved.

Scripture quotations marked NIV are taken from the THE HOLY BIBLE, NEW INTERNATIONAL VERSION®, NIV® Copyright © 1973, 1978, 1984, 2011 by Biblica, Inc.™ Used by permission. All rights reserved worldwide.

Scripture quotations marked KJV are taken from the King James Version of the Bible.

Copyright © 2013 David Litwin
All rights reserved.
ISBN: 978-0615943190

For Cindy, Randi and Rachel

CONTENTS

CONTENTS 5
IN IT TO WIN IT 9
A FAITH OF ASSIGNMENTS 15
THE "UNFULFILLED ASSIGNMENT" 21
RETHINKING THE KINGDOM: 25
THE "RE" WORDS 31
THE ROYAL SITE SURVEYOR 37
THE SOUL CANISTER 45
DEMSTIFYING THE MYSTIC 51
BECOMING LIKE CHRIST (IN ACTION AND NATURE) 59
BECOMING SPIRIT "LISTENERS" 63
THE GRACIOUSNESS OF THE SPIRIT 67
THE POWER OF "SECOND BREATH" 71
THE UNBREAKABLE CODE 79
INTERCESSION… WITHOUT CEASING 87
THINKING BEYOND THE "CHURCH LADY" 93

SARCASM – THE THICKENING	97
FOCUSING ON SPIRIT "PHENOMENA"	105
(SELF) "RIGHTEOUS" ANGER	109
THE BODY BATTLE:	113
THE "STRATEGY" OF SIN	119
LEARNING TO LIVE "ON MISSION"	127
ON MISSION: EMPATHY	131
ON MISSION: NOT KOOKY	135
ON MISSION: LISTEN MORE, TALK LESS	137
ON MISSION: PRE-FALL EVANGELISM	141
ON MISSION: RELATIONSHIP MOMENTUM	145
ACTIVATING KINGDOM ACTION	151
THE FINAL FORMULA	159
ACKNOWLEDGEMENTS	167

CHAPTER 1

IN IT TO WIN IT

I'm not a runner. I often joke with others that I can barely run water. I work out in other ways, but I have little desire to run. I'm sure that if a doctor to tell me that I was on the verge of high cholesterol or diabetes, I might think differently. In this immediate moment however, without much motivation, running doesn't occupy my time. Perhaps I could say, based on the painful requirements necessary to be a runner, I have little *incentive* to run.

Now imagine yourself in my running shoes. Suppose a personal trainer were to come to you and state that if you were to spend the next six months rigorously training, radically changing your eating habits, and shaving out most of your leisure time that he could guarantee that you would place in the top 100 runners in your local turkey trot.

10 MISSION

Would you do it? No offense to the turkey trot, but it is highly unlikely you would alter your lifestyle for such a nominal reward.

What if that same trainer could guarantee that, after that same six months, you would win the Boston Marathon and receive all the fame and prestige that went with it? Would that alter your response? You would be assured of superstar status and a multi-million dollar NIKE deal. Did *that* change your mind? Every day spent in brutal endurance training and radical dieting would be coated in the knowledge that, in just a few months, your life would be transformed forever.

What changed between the local trot and the international marathon? Your body would still need to endure the same painful experiences. Your life would still be radically hijacked for a few months, and your social time would drop to near nil. Wouldn't the reward from the latter event be worth the endurance necessary to receive it?

With the preceding in mind, I would like to propose a question.

Why, with all the Christians in America, have we not made more of an impact on this modern American culture?

In the book of Acts, when the governmental leaders spoke of the early disciples, they referred to those men and women as the ones, "turning the world upside down." Can we make the same declaration today? Think about it for a second. If the Bible is true, then we serve the most potent Force in the universe, the Epitome and Creator of love and humanity. Why hasn't that impact reached every facet of this society? In fact, we could say that in many areas of culture, both geographically and sociologically, Christianity has lost considerable ground.

Oh, sure, we can blame the media, modernist progressive ideologies, the radical left wing, or our secular academic institutions. We can cite a rise in Eastern mysticism and new age religions, secular high-court appointments, or the embrace of tolerance. We can even go after other denominations that don't think the way we do and so are polluting the truth of God's Word. We have book upon book and radio pundits galore that are locked and loaded, ready to play the blame game. We consider the answer to Christianity's eroding brand image to be outside of ourselves instead of searching inside.

To quote my favorite singer songwriter, Jack Johnson:

I doubt I'm gonna win you back
When you got eyes like that
They won't let me in
Always <u>looking out</u>
Jack Johnson, *If I had Eyes*

What if the answer is the same reason I am not a runner? What if it's an issue of *incentive*? Remember the reasons I would consider running. A health scare or a life altering victory were my two motivating factors. In many ways, we treat our Christian life the same way. Once I become a believer, I'm in. I'm secure. Metaphorically, I've already won the Boston Marathon and so much more. That's true, but it's a guarantee in the future, one that was previously paid for by Christ. In other words, it's like the trainer coming to you and stating, "I can

12 MISSION

guarantee that in six months you will win the Boston Marathon," but guess what?

You don't have to do a thing to achieve it.

What's your incentive then? Well, you could say, " I should train," and give it some effort because it's the 'right thing' to do. Perhaps you would train out of guilt, a sense of empathy, or justice, but would you exert the same level of effort and rigor to the training if the reward were already guaranteed?

Now again, regardless of the assurance of a marathon win, if you were to suffer from a heart attack or diabetes, I can imagine that you would grab those running shoes and hit the pavement. In the case of the health scare, we train because of negatively impacting circumstances. Think about it, don't we often discipline ourselves in our faith, only to gradually start to wane, but then pick our spiritual disciplines back up once trials and struggles resurface in our lives?

Our spiritual discipline often fluctuates depending on our circumstances, and motivation can seem difficult when our salvation is secure. We often become Christians without *internal* zeal and momentum. For some reason, however, we are still wonderfully adept at *external* assessment and judgment. All the external forces pushing against Christianity aside, I think this is part of our brand problem.

I believe there is a solution.

This book was written because I am confident that there is an opportunity in Christianity that is so wondrous, so winsome, and so life altering that it is worth the discipline one must undergo to realize it. The best part is that it is available right now. It's not something in the future, and not something we need to feel obligated or scared into adopting. I believe that its adoption and practice can radically turn Christianity's brand problem around in an instant.

In the coming chapters, I will give you a Mission. Actually, I show you a Mission. It's nothing revolutionarily new. It's nothing that you haven't read in scripture before. You simply may not have understood its significance. I believe that when you see it, when you lock in to how you have been designed as a believer to be part of it, you will never be the same. Hopefully, better yet, the world will never be the same.

CHAPTER 2:

A FAITH OF ASSIGNMENTS

We know that God has given us assignments as born-again believers. For example, Jesus stated that we are to *"make disciples of all nations, baptizing them in the name of the Father, the Son and the Holy Spirit."* (Matt. 28:19 NIV) We are told to sanctify ourselves, to devote ourselves to teaching and prayer, and to have fellowship with other believers. We are also called to be like Christ.

We are told, somewhat extra biblically, that we need to be in a church building on Sundays and possibly on Wednesdays, and no doubt to frequent a bible study sometime during the other days of the week. We may even have been told we should listen to and watch

16 MISSION

Christian-based media and we are encouraged not to drink, smoke, or chew, or go out with girls or guys that do.

Why?

Extra-biblical standards aside, why do we do these things Jesus and the Bible commands? You might say we do them because God commands us, and because we love Him, we obey his commandments. Since the Bible not only contains a list of "do's," but also quite a few "don'ts," we then can say we DON'T do certain things because God commands us NOT to do them. We love Him, so we obey His commandments. While true, focusing *solely* on that mindset can take God's love out of the equation.

Imagine you have a four-year-old daughter. One day, she ventures into the kitchen just as you are boiling pasta and cooking sausage on the stove. As she gets closer to the hot appliance, you reach out, grab her hand, and say, "don't get near the stove!" You've given her a rather forceful command. It is not based on the stove or your subjugating will. It's based on love. You don't want your precious daughter to get burned.

I would hope that sometime around the age of eight or nine, you would bring your daughter into the kitchen, explain how to use the stove, and reveal to her the joy of cooking. In other words, you would help her understand why you had been so dogmatic about the stove for all those years. She was too young to fully grasp your firm commands.

Now imagine never having that talk with your daughter.

At age forty, she's still afraid to go near the stove because all her life, "daddy told her not to." And for four decades, she obeyed you out of love for her dad.

Are you a good father?

Eventually, as she watched all the others around her enjoying culinary delights in the kitchen while she sat in the corner and was possibly mocked by her peers, wouldn't resentment start to well up? As a father, you want your child to understand the "why" of your commands; you don't want him or her to follow your will blindly.

Yet, when it comes to our Christian walk, we often fail to ask those very questions. We chalk it up to a term that we use as Christians: "faith." We don't need to know the answer to "why." After all, "God said it, I believe it, and that settles it." Like the 40 year old, with faith to believe that Daddy simply knows best, the world mocks and scoffs, calls us out of date and out of touch, turning our belief system into media and mainstream mockery. Every year, our light in this culture appears to grow dimmer. Look what God says about this type of reasoning:

> *"Because this people draw near with their words*
> *And honor Me with their lip service,*
> *But they remove their hearts far from Me,*
> <u>*And their reverence for Me consists of tradition learned by rote,"*</u>
> Isa. 29:13 NASB (emphasis mine)

18 MISSION

Getting a little more current, I believe that the condition of much of the church in our modern culture can best be summed up in the lyrics from a classic Christian rock song from the Australian band, The Newsboys. Let these lyrics sink in as you read:

LOST THE PLOT

When you come back again
Would you bring me something from the fridge?
Heard a rumor that the end is near
But I just got comfortable here.
Sigh.
Let's be blunt.
I'm a little distracted.
What do you want?
Once we could follow,
Now we cannot.
You would not fit our image,
So we lost the plot.

Once we could hear you,
Now our senses are shot.
We've forgotten our first love.
We have lost the plot.

Are you still listening?
'Cause we're obviously not
We've forgotten our first love
We have lost the plot.

And why are you still calling?
You forgave, we forgot.
We're such experts at stalling
That we've lost the plot.
Lost the plot

I am confident that one of the prevailing reasons we haven't made God's intended impact on our culture today is that we follow God without asking the "why" questions. We know inherently that we need to embody Godly characteristics, but our answer is often because we "need to embody Godly characteristics."

I believe that our actions, our obedience, and our disciplines are not simply to be practiced because God told us to, and not just because we love His words and take them on faith. Each of God's micro-commands is part of a macro-intention. Like the secular scientists of today, we create a sort of reductionist Christianity, thinking that it's not all related. We don't connect the dots.

Because we don't connect the dots, we often fail to live intentional Christian lives, and we certainly aren't very connected to each other. We segment our church bodies, we inoculate ourselves from the visions and passions of other congregations. We remain content to fulfill our own missions, separate from the supposedly like-minded communities around us.

In the next chapter, we will start to connect the dots. You'll be shown a Mission, an unfinished assignment. It doesn't belong to a single denominational group. It was not given to a select few. What

20 MISSION

makes this mission so special and so life-altering, is that it's not YOUR assignment, at least not until you start becoming like Christ. That revelation changes and impacts everything.

CHAPTER 3:

THE "UNFULFILLED ASSIGNMENT"

To understand this unfulfilled assignment, to grasp the Mission, we begin with a conversation. It's a heavenly conversation found in the book of Psalms – chapter 110 to be exact.

> *The LORD says to my Lord: "Sit at My right hand until I make all Your enemies a footstool for Your feet."*
> Ps.110:1, NASB

This little passage is one of the most quoted scriptures from the Old Testament to the New Testament. That's interesting, isn't it? There must be some serious significance to this verse for it to be mentioned in Mark, Matthew, Luke, I Corinthians, Hebrews, and Acts.

22 THE "UNFULFILLED ASSIGNMENT"

Let's break this verse down. In the heavenly conversation of the verse above, you have a dialog between two parties.

THE LORD (God) said to MY LORD (Jesus), "Sit at My right hand until I make Your enemies a footstool for Your feet."

We see in this conversation that God has given His Son, Jesus Christ, a command: "Sit at My right hand..." Until what?

"Until I make all Your enemies a footstool for Your feet."

If we make this verse our mission, then our lives should reflect a desire to make all of God's enemies Christ's footstool. We live to eradicate God's enemies. We hate what He hates and we love what He loves. We often do this through spiritual, social, moral, and even political means. This puts quite a weight of responsibility on us. If it's our job, then we often attack things *and people* that we feel are "against God. While we forget, or ignore, that pesky little passage: *"our battle is not with flesh and blood..."*

In this book I am going to postulate that we've gotten it wrong. What if it's not one of our assignments?

Let's go back to the passage again:

The LORD (God) said to <u>MY</u> Lord (Jesus), "Sit at My right hand until I make Your enemies a footstool for Your feet."

THE "UNFULFILLED ASSIGNMENT"   23

This "MY" would imply that we have a third party present in the conversation, so who is this mysterious heavenly party crasher? Let's be literal for a second. We have to keep in mind that this was written by David in Psalms, so perhaps he is speaking allegorically.

In the moment, it was the Lord (God), My Lord (Jesus), and then whatever party was present to document the statement. Who was this third party? Well, it's a heavenly conversation so naturally we can assume that if God is Father, Son, and Spirit, then the Spirit would be our mysterious third listener. We can assume this, but it becomes wholly concrete when we come to this verse in the New Testament, a verse that sheds full clarity on our heavenly party crasher:

> David himself said <u>in the Holy Spirit,</u> "The Lord said to my Lord, 'Sit at My right hand, until I put Your enemies beneath Your feet.'" Mark 12:36, NASB (emphasis added)

Now we have it confirmed! David, channeling, if you will, the Holy Spirit, recited what the Holy Spirit witnessed. We can look at it this way:

"Sit at my right hand" was God's order.

The order to "sit" was given to Jesus, but "make Your enemies a footstool" was the assignment.

It wasn't an assignment, or Mission, given to mankind, or even to born-again humanity. It was given to the Holy Spirit.

24 THE "UNFULFILLED ASSIGNMENT"

It is not an assignment you could take on. It's an assignment of and for the Kingdom.

CHAPTER 4:

RETHINKING THE KINGDOM:

The term 'Kingdom' has been somewhat of a nebulous term in Christendom. For centuries, the term has been synonymous with heaven. "When we come into the Kingdom (Heaven), what a glorious day that will be," is often the church's mindset. In the last century, we began talking about the Kingdom as the work that God is doing on Earth through His believers *until* we get to Heaven. Therefore, as Christians, we are now a part of the Kingdom, and everything we do after that moment of salvation is Kingdom-related. In so doing, we've even associated the Kingdom with why we should get a discount from the local Christian merchant: "I might not pay you what you are worth, but remember, *it's for the Kingdom*, brother."

26 MISSION

In the last couple of decades, the church has shifted to a different understanding of the Kingdom: The Kingdom is not just our future home, but that it is also here now. Better yet, that it is *available now*. It goes by the term "Kingdom Now" theology. This is a far more relevant and mission oriented concept, but often that "Kingdom Now" mission is crafted morally and politically. In other words, it's our mission again. We are responsible for building the Kingdom of God, just like we think we are responsible for placing all of God's enemies under Christ's feet.

What is wrong with this train of thought? After all, we are building for the glory of God? There's just one problem; we can't know the Kingdom. Consider Jesus' prayer in Matthew 6:

> *"Our father, who is in heaven, hallowed be Your name. Your Kingdom come. Your will be done. On earth AS IT IS IN HEAVEN."*
> Matthew 6:9-10 NASB (emphasis mine)

Therein lies the dilemma. Apart from a lucky few that have died and come back to tell about it, none of us have been to heaven. We can know, in principle, the attributes of Heaven, but we don't know the general dynamics, the essential makeup of heaven itself. Where do we go to learn Kingdom dynamics?

We go back to the beginning.

Let's do a brief Scriptural survey for a moment. Starting in Genesis, we learn that in the beginning, when the earth was "formless and void," God looked over the void and said, *"Let there be light."* In the next six "days," God crafted out the wonder of the universe, providentially birthing the planets and stars, the plants and animals, and mankind itself. Placing him in the perfection of God's Garden, God spoke to man, telling him and his offspring to be "fruitful and multiply." His new human creation was given its first commandment, to "fill the earth, and subdue it. "

That mission didn't last long, as the antagonist in this story, the enemy of God and mankind (played at first by a serpent) tricked the first humans into disobeying God and then in shame, blaming each other, God, and the serpent for their error. They were kicked out of the paradise of the Earth, or "Eden," forced to endure a life of bondage and toil. God cursed both man and the earth. For generations, this difficult life of toil, desolation, and destruction continued until God's people, now referred to as "Israelites," were enslaved by another group: the Egyptians.

Thankfully, this enslaved group was rescued from slavery and subjugation through a former prince of Egypt, a man named Moses. Moses, who was actually a member of the Israelites by birth, led the people out of bondage and into a new land that God had promised to them.

Along the way, God gave this group, these "Israelites," a set of statutes to follow, beginning with His ten commandments. For the next few millennia, these Israelites would adopt and discard these commandments depending on their economic, agricultural, or spiritual condition or the zeal of the king or prophet leading them.

28 MISSION

Many nations rose and fell during this time, but at the highpoint of one of these empires, the Roman Empire, a Man stepped onto the scene. He was immediately seen as a dissident by the Roman leadership and a heretic by the Israeli religious leaders because this Man claimed to be the Son of the God of the Israelites, and all mankind. He led a ministry for about three years, gaining a massive following and garnering a small select few into His inner circle. His ministry was filled with miraculous circumstances and providentially profound sermons and stories. Sadly, his life was cut short. Those religious leaders who were losing influence and the officials of Rome who were concerned with rebellion killed this Man by hanging Him on a cross.

This wasn't the end for this Man, for three days later, He rose again, conquering the death that was determined to hold Him, and proclaiming the power of His resurrection. Through His death and resurrection, man was given access to a "born again" life, and the entrance into eternal life. In regard to the Mission, when Jesus left, ascending into heaven, He "breathed" on them in the Spirit, saying of His previous miraculous works: *"greater things than these will you do."* For the next few decades, his ragtag group of disciples "turned the world upside down," until many were killed by the religious leaders or the Roman government.

Chances are, you know this story. But here's the new revelation. It's found in the following verse:

"Jesus Christ is the same, yesterday, today and forever."
Heb 13:8 NASB (emphasis mine)

If God is "the same, yesterday today and forever," then His <u>first</u> intent is always his intended intent.

Let's say that my nature never changes. As an unchanging person, let's suppose that I have a ten-year-old daughter, and I decide she should become a ballerina. Everything I do from that moment forward is to steer her toward becoming a ballerina. From taking her to the ballet, to signing her up for dance classes, to encouraging her to associate with other dancers, I am 100% focused on this intent for my daughter. She may have her own will and want to become an astronaut or a policewoman. If my will never changes, despite her independent desires, I am always trying to steer her back towards becoming a ballerina. Her will may fluctuate, but mine does not. My first intent is still my intended intent for my daughter.

Although we see all things as a progression toward Christ, if God doesn't change, then Christ is *also* part of the progression back to God's original intent for humanity, the time before the fall of man. It is the time when those on Earth and those in heaven were in a symbiotic relationship.

> *"Your Kingdom come. Your will be done. <u>On earth</u> as it is in heaven."*
> Matthew 6:10 NASB (emphasis mine)

Heaven becomes an integral component in the Mission, but the Mission itself circles back to God's first actions, a pre-fall (before the sin of Adam) Earth and a perfect relationship between God and man in the here and now, not in the by and by. It is a time when, once again, God's enemies are placed under Christ's feet.

CHAPTER 5:

THE "RE" WORDS

If we hypothesize that God's first action is always His intended action, then we can search the scriptures for validation to this declaration. We find them in the "RE" words scattered throughout the New Testament. Notice the words that are used by Christ and His apostles, especially after they received the Spirit.

REdemption
REconciliation
REnewal
REgeneration
Restoration

32 MISSION

These words reference BACK to something in the past, and, in God's case, something intended. For example, we are not called to make our minds new - we are called to "renew" our minds. "Renewal" unveils that we are not becoming something new, but that we are bringing our minds back into their *intended state of being*. The "RE" words define and describe God's intentions. Take, for example, the term "*reconciliation.*"

> *All this is from God, who reconciled us to himself through Christ and gave us the <u>ministry of reconciliation</u>: that God was reconciling the world to himself in Christ, not counting people's sins against them. And he has committed to us the <u>message of reconciliation</u>.*
> 2 Cor. 5:18-19, NIV (emphasis mine)

Reconciliation is a term that predominantly has remained a religious distinction. The idea of a "ministry of reconciliation," under its common guise, refers to the bringing together of different people groups and societies to recognize past hurts and offenses. In addition, it often is mentioned in the context of "reconciling" man back to God – or the redemption of man back to his Creator. Although these are crucial and critical parts of the Christian walk, the natural definition of the term exposes an even greater and deeper purpose.

Reconciliation is a *banking term.*

Remember that thing before Internet banking called a check register? It predominantly grew extinct in our digital age. Back in the day, your checkbook contained a few pages of unfilled-out, gridded lines right at the front of the book. This was called a register. That register was supposed to be filled with all of your previous transactions: the money you had withdrawn from your account as well as the monetary deposits you had added. At the far right of the columns was a section entitled "total" where you would tally the "supposed" amount of money still left in your bank account at the time of the last withdrawal or deposit.

I say "supposed" amount, because you couldn't be certain that the number in your register actually matched the correct amount of money stored at your bank. You would contact your bank to get your official balance, in order to ensure that the amount written in your register matched the amount the bank actually held. If these two numbers matched, you were then said to have "reconciled" your account.

Let's break this down. There are two parts described above: the money that you personally calculated in your register and the money the bank actually held. If the money in the bank was the real number, we could say that the amount in the bank was "perfect." It was the true and real amount of money you had acquired. Your register contained some derivation of that perfect number. When you finally matched up those two numbers, the derivation and the perfect merged.

This is the call of the Creator, the prayer of Jesus in Matthew 6 and the Spirit's Mission: To take the derivation in our current world and reconcile it back to the perfect. God is perfect in Spirit, Love, and Truth, but mankind and existence, since the fall of man, are in the state of derivation. As man bows to the lure of sin and suffers sin's intended biological, psychological, societal, generational, and yes, spiritual

34 MISSION

outcomes, that derivation becomes a grosser and grosser distortion of the original. God's perfect plan is further disrupted and agitated and the intended prosperity and purpose of humanity is stagnated. God's plan always has been the perfect, humanity and the world in its pre-fall state (before the sin of Adam). Despite the actuality of our post-fall world, the perfect remains the purpose.

> *"Your Kingdom come. Your will be done. On earth (the derivation) as it is in heaven (the perfect)."*
> Matthew 6:10 NASB (parentheses mine)

It is through seeing what is extinct in the perfect that displays what we must do in the derivation.

For example, there is no disease in the perfect; therefore, we must do whatever we can to eliminate disease from the derivation. We can do this through more aggressive understanding and treatments of diseases, recognizing them as strategies and not merely unintended outcomes. We can recognize that the Creator has crafted His vegetative and animal creation to help stave off diseases and complications, and begin to broadcast in more fervent ways the benefits of embracing less-processed food diets. We also can do so through real and documented healings.

There is no judgment in the perfect; so we can put down our moralistic bullhorns and love others simply as God's creation; despite ideological, religious and sexual orientations. There is no fear and destruction in the perfect, so we can begin to encourage and petition our media channels to more regularly broadcast the atrocities going on in other parts of the world, and we can come together with those of all faiths to attempt to alleviate the pain and suffering across the globe. There is no hate or selfish comparison in the perfect, so we consciously can chose to love and accept those that look, act, and believe differently than we do.

There is no sin or its byproduct in the perfect, so we can begin to broadcast the *strategies of sin* to humanity and expose the enemy of mankind's purposeful intent. We will discuss that more in the coming chapters.

Jesus is the bridge between the fallen world and God's original intention. He is, therefore, the "New Adam." He brought God's intent back to the earth to be realized through His "children," or saved and "born again" humanity. Remember Jesus' declaration, *"the Kingdom of Heaven is at hand?"* God's intent was wholly manifested through Christ. In every action He committed, Jesus was focused on the Mission. His life and death were both central to the Mission, and the impetus of its completion. God's son started the Mission; God's children, His "heirs," are to finish it.

But we weren't to finish it alone. We were given a helper:

I will ask the Father, and He will give you another **Helper**, *that He may be with you forever;*
John 14:15-17 NASB

36 MISSION

If we read this scripture outside of the Mission, then the Spirit's role is often to help us in our daily struggles and opportunities as we make our way toward Heaven. If we see this scripture in light of the Mission, then we are also here to help the Spirit with His assignment. We are integral partners with the Spirit for the sake of the Mission, because He can't complete it alone. The next chapter will provide us a story to help better understand how the Spirit operates in His Kingdom role.

CHAPTER 6:

THE ROYAL SITE SURVEYOR

Why did Jesus promise the disciples that after His ascension the Holy Spirit would follow, and that it would be better that He came? There are of course numerous theological reasons, but there is one overarching reason that may have yet to be presented. It becomes a central reason for the blessings that accompany the Holy Spirit. The answer is so simple and so non-spiritual that it has been likely skipped over for millennia:

He's been in heaven.

Imagine that you are the royal site surveyor of a kingdom on a beautiful island in the tropics. It is an island of paradise, beauty and

38 MISSION

ease. Everything at the king's disposal also is available to you. The finest luxuries are within the grasp of your pampered fingertips. In fact, the island itself is its own greatest treasure. The cool tropical breezes blow softly through your large estate as you daily sit and dine on the best royal cuisine in the kingdom, recurrently watching the sun slip down past the ocean horizon in swathes of orange and violet. Resting back in your soft, luxurious chair, you cross your arms behind your neck and think, "I never want to leave this place."

Then one day your monarch summons you to his side. He instructs you to go to an island with none of the beauty, elegance, or utopian elements of your island home. It is an island of dust and bramble; little there compares to your beautiful residence. Still, your monarch feels that the land has immense value and he wants to renovate it. The stipulation is that you must remain on that island until you finish topologically surveying the last square inch of the island. After you complete your assignment, you may come home.

Having full knowledge and memory of your true island paradise, but cordoned on that destitute island until you are finished, would you lackadaisically meander around? Or would you attempt to complete the project as quickly as possible so you could return to your island paradise? Of course, you would work quickly, for the place you currently find yourself is where your monarch has placed you, not where you reside. The current residence cannot hold a candle to your real home. Your stay is not a condition of time, but of action. You have a task to do; complete it, and you get to come home.

In the same way, this is why the Holy Spirit becomes such a value to the Earth. God created the universe and humanity and rested. Jesus was slain on a cross for our sins, and said, "It is finished." The Holy Spirit is responsible for bringing the Kingdom, or God's intent for humanity and the earth, and that is an unfulfilled assignment. Moreover, as we have discovered, Jesus has been instructed not to return until that assignment, the Mission, has been carried out:

Those who might have lived in the destitute land where the royal site surveyor was stationed may not have understood why this man was so adamant about getting his job completed. After all, they had existed quite nicely on the meager provisions the land provided. They had survived at least, hadn't they? Why was this man so eager to leave their homestead, that to them was all there was? Because he'd been in paradise, he knew what it looked like. He'd walked along the crystal blue water's edge, bathed in the tropical glow on the veranda of his palatial estate and enjoyed fruit and drink of immense culinary delight. He worked quickly because he wanted to return home.

Now let's suppose people on that island started listening to that royal site surveyor. Perhaps maybe a few generations before, they had been given a book that described his wondrous home. Though all they had known was their own meager existence, perhaps some of them considered that maybe this place that they hadn't seen, that this man claimed to have come from, was far better than where they were living. If they were to come to him and inquire about going back to his island paradise with him, what do you suppose his response would be? Would he say no, and continue the task alone, taking years upon years before returning?

40 MISSION

Or would he say, "Come help me?"

The site surveyor knew what his contractual job was: to survey the entire land. With help, he could complete his job quicker and return home. The more that believed and joined, the faster the task would be completed. He also knew that he himself was the outsider; it would be far better for them to recruit others to complete the task from their own group. For those early joiners he would pour out story upon story of his home, so that they could tell their circle of acquaintances about his home from their own mouths and recruit more and more people to help in the task. Once he finished his task, the site surveyor made the journey home and with him came all those who helped in the process.

That is where the wisdom of the king had come into play. In his love and benevolence, he *wanted* the inhabitants of that destitute island nation to come and live on his island paradise. However, he didn't want to force them, so he used his royal site surveyor to accomplish his always-intended desire...

And this gospel of the kingdom will be preached in the whole world as a testimony to all nations, and then the end will come.
Matt. 24:14, NIV

This is a perfect example of the Holy Spirit and yet an imperfect one. It is similar because it accurately describes why God would have sent His Holy Spirit. It is imperfect because in the scenario above the royal site surveyor existed in tangible form alongside the islanders. It also vividly proves why the enemy has kept mankind away from the

Holy Spirit, and why mankind must embrace the Holy Spirit to accomplish God's intended task. Because the Holy Spirit operates through a creation to whom God gave free will. He also most often lies dormant inside of any creation that does not first accept that God exists and that He sent His son to die for mankind's salvation. His dormancy or activation is tied to the winsomeness and attractiveness of those claiming to serve Christ. That attractiveness and winsomeness is a direct result of whether they have accepted the process of sanctification through which the Holy Spirit is given entrance, as you will discover in the next few chapters.

The Holy Spirit is one of the most hotly contested concepts in all of theology, and here we see why. It is His assignment of Kingdom recreation that Jesus prayed in Matthew 6: "Thy Kingdom come, thy will be done, on earth as it is in Heaven." He understands the plans and He knows all the objectives. Too often, we try to take the Word into our own hands instead of letting the Spirit guide us. It hasn't done us much good; the world still looks like the dusty, brambly land it always has resembled since the fall of man. Instead, we must partner with the Site Surveyor and in so doing, help in fulfilling the King's ultimate agenda.

You have now been shown how the Holy Spirit operates according to the Mission. Now it is time to see the integral role you play in its fulfillment.

42 MISSION

EPILOGUE:

I originally wrote this story years ago after feeling called by God to write about a "Royal Site Surveyor." I had absolutely no idea what I was going write. I simply sat down at the computer and let the words Providentially flow into my fingers and onto the computer screen. What you now have read is what came out of that exercise. It was written eight years before this book ever became an idea.

Note that the request was to write about a SURVEYOR. It was a few weeks after writing the story that God brought me to the passage below. I had never read or understood it from this context before, but note the precise wording in the text. I believe that this prophetic passage is a picture of the Spirit and how He views this home versus His home of paradise. I have to say that I marveled at God's sovereignty and precision after I read this. I've underlined key words in this passage for emphasis.

"Who has <u>measured</u> the waters in the hollow of his hand,

or with the breadth of his hand <u>marked off</u> the heavens?

Who has held the <u>dust of the earth</u> in a basket,

or <u>weighed the mountains on the scales</u>

and the hills in a balance?

Who can fathom the <u>Spirit of the Lord</u>,

or instruct the Lord as his counselor?

Whom did the Lord consult to enlighten him,

and who taught him the right way?

Who was it that taught him knowledge,

or showed him the path of understanding?

Surely <u>the nations are like a drop in a bucket</u>;

<u>they are regarded as dust on the scales</u>;

<u>he weighs the islands</u> as though they were fine dust.

Lebanon is not sufficient for altar fires,

nor its animals enough for burnt offerings.

<u>Before him all the nations are as nothing</u>;

<u>they are regarded by him as worthless</u>

<u>and less than nothing</u>."

Isa. 40: 12-17 NIV (emphasis mine)

CHAPTER 7:

THE SOUL CANISTER

A few years back I found myself wrestling with how one person could hear the truth of the gospel and respond immediately, but another could hear the same message and yet it would fall on deaf ears. If each person is spirit, soul, and body, how was it that a person's spirit might fail to be provoked when introduced to spiritual things? I figured it was a decent enough question to bring back to the Maker of it all. On a typical Sunday afternoon I asked God rather non-expectantly, "What is the relationship between the body, soul, and spirit?" The answer came back almost instantaneously:

"The soul is the canister."

It was an unusual metaphor, and I am not one to merely assume I have heard a word and "proclaim it from the rooftops" without serious evaluation. Through that evaluation, and the subsequent meditation, many aspects and verses of the faith burst forth far clearer. Validating this statement would be nearly impossible. Instead, I will start with the presupposition that the soul's functions as the canister and work the argument backward from that hypothesis.

If the soul is the canister, scripture asserts it can contain two entities: the Spirit and the flesh. Scripturally, "flesh" is any aspect of our self-identity and character that intentionally or unintentionally sets itself up against God and, more importantly, His purposes. "Flesh" doesn't always have to be blatant sin. It can be fear, insecurity, doubt, anger, jealousy, success, stress, or a combination of a myriad of other prideful qualities that we either act out of, or avoid action because of. Some of our soul canister's "fleshly" content rises through our own actions. Other aspects of flesh are thrust on us through the actions of others. Regardless of the method of insertion, the contents of the canister help incite our actions, coat our beliefs, and determine our future visions. Though this flesh reference is common, especially in evangelistic settings, the canister metaphor unveils a deeper discovery.

Though *"all have sinned and fallen short of the glory of God,"* the level of flesh in the canister and its method of insertion can vary from person to person.

Prior to salvation, the canister is solely filled with flesh proportionate to whatever level a person's previous actions and/or circumstances might have dictated. At the moment of salvation, through repentance and acceptance of Christ, the canister is penetrated by God through His Holy Spirit. Most denominations claim the indwelling of the Spirit, though how He indwells is often the subject of heated debate. Using the canister metaphor, we can postulate that at salvation, the Holy Spirit imprints Himself on the soul canister. The person's soul is a "new creation." Often, flesh still garners most of the liquid mass. Like a bottle of Dom Perignon filled with turpentine regardless of the amount of brackish liquid contained inside, the "ownership" and "identity" of the bottle remains constant.

We can use this metaphor to deepen our clarity of the **role of the sanctification process** in the life of a believer. It is the Spirit's job, through the willing participation of the new believer, to increase His volume in the canister. Sanctification is the process of draining fleshly content and replacing it with Spiritual volume and in so doing becoming more and more like Christ.

Christ, in human form, is the ultimate example of a man wholly devoid of flesh while wholly filled with the Spirit. Meaning, we are called to be like Christ, not just in action – *but also in His nature.*

Using the same metaphor, we can expose the antithesis. While the Spirit attempts to remove flesh and exponentially increase His volume in the canister, the enemy of humanity uses every spiritual, social, sexual, technological, egotistical, or diversionary device at his disposal to push against any rising spiritual content and gain back volume percentage for the flesh. Should the Christian give in to these tactics the Spirit in the believer often relinquishes ground back to the flesh. This exposes another hidden reality: One can be a theological giant, a multi-decade evangelist, a powerful worship leader, or a pastor of a megachurch and be horribly losing this flesh/Spirit battle through a myriad of means. The church is replete with members and leaders that are theologically stuffed, morally militant, flesh dominated… and Spirit anemic.

This is in part because the sanctification process has been largely recast into "discipleship." Discipleship, however, has become programmatic and/or gauged with performance metrics. Rather than focusing on the removal of flesh and the insertion of Spirit, discipleship often entails going through a particular Christian book or area of scripture. As the group progresses, the head facilitator often looks for those that rise to the top both in personality and knowledge of the Word. Those budding "leaders" are then equipped to become the heads of new discipleship groups and so on and so forth.

The mindset to discipleship can cause churches to bury some of God's greatest jewels. In the new members class of a church I previously attended, there was a woman whose fleshly canister content was largely caused by the many tragedies inflicted on her in her past. Her canister content manifested itself in a fear of praying out loud, a byproduct of years of unmerciful verbal abuse by men in her life. The very reason for the onslaught of fear was that her canister already was primed for Spirit activation; she had done little volitionally to add fleshly content. Her prayers soon would have moved mountains; there was little of her to get in the way.

In contrast, my canister was a large seething cauldron of flesh I had spent decades personally heightening. I hid my canister's contents behind a dynamic personality, a "can-do" attitude and decent oration skills. Instead of recognizing the difference between our two canisters, I was repeatedly elevated, despite the lack of flesh removal. Tragically, she was cast aside, labeled as "unwilling" to participate in God's "command" of praying out loud. Thankfully, what the church failed to do, God did in my life through His own sanctification process. But when this woman finally left that church shortly before I did, there was new flesh in her canister, inserted by the very people claiming to represent Christ.

> *If anyone causes one of these little ones—those who believe in me—to stumble, it would be better for them to have a large millstone hung around their neck and to be drowned in the depths of the sea.*
> Matt. 18:6, NIV

Hers was a story of tragic outcome, not volitional action. But if the Spirit loses considerable ground due to backslidden actions of the believer, the canister may once again become so filled with flesh that the flesh pushes back against the final layer of Spirit imprinting. At this moment before cessation, the Spirit often will shock the canister in hopes of staging a reversal. Testimony after testimony of the backsliding believer contains nearly identical scenarios: at the apex of rebellion and running from God, some thought, conversation, or circumstance jolts the wayward pilgrim back to the reality of his or her actions, and he or she once again returns to the path of the righteous. Prodigal after prodigal returns out of what often is called the "dark night of the soul."

50 MISSION

Through the canister metaphor, we have given further clarity to sanctification and uncloaked the agenda of the enemy. By continuing down this metaphorical path we can delve far deeper to: demystify the mystic, disclose a critical mission of the Spirit, and determine the right metrics to distinguish the false from the real.

CHAPTER 8:

DEMSTIFYING THE MYSTIC

Since the Protestant Reformation, apart from a small microcosm of the Christian populous, the terms "Christian" and "mystic" have been systematically separated. Thankfully, through the metaphor of the canister, these two terms not only begin to re-fuse, but the term "mystic" can be demystified in the process. If the soul is the canister, where either flesh or Spirit dwells, then through the humble process of sanctification, the believer, while decreasing flesh, increases the volume of the Spirit. If the soul canister is taking in more spiritual volume, and that canister resides inside the body of the believer, then through the sanctification process the believer should daily become more connected with the Holy Spirit than with the flesh.

52 MISSION

Put another way, I logically should become more of a mystical being through every stage of the sanctification process. God's Spirit inside of me increases through my willingness to engage in the extraction of flesh, through repentance, humility, prayer and scriptural devotion. Through humble sanctification, not strident asceticism, I am becoming more Spirit because my soul, the core of my body, is being taken over by His essence. As the volume of the Spirit increases and the volume of the flesh decreases, and I am more indwelled by the Spirit, then logically I should be able to operate according to the traits of the Spirit, provided I actively am pursuing this process. Sanctification creates, and demystifies, the mystic. In becoming like Christ, we become greater receptacles for His Essence.

This shatters some current presuppositions about the path of the Christian mystic. Through the canister metaphor, we discover that the denial of the body is not the same as the extraction of the flesh. If the metaphor is true, then asceticism may be the path for those to whom gluttony and comfort have translated into fleshly content, but it cannot be THE path. We each have different levels of flesh in our canisters, as well as different methods for its insertion, so the path of extraction must be walked in humble partnership with the Spirit, not necessarily through the suffering of the body.

In addition, Monastic isolation may not be the correct path, for properly self-evaluating one's sanctification progress requires placing oneself around the very circumstances pressing against transformation. It is easy to claim to be a man or woman of patience or chastity if all circumstances requiring patience or sexual temptation are eliminated.

This adds further illumination to the scriptural idea: *"Be in the world, but not of it."* It may be that being "in" the world is a key factor in extracting flesh from our canisters. Could it be that the Spirit echoes along with James, *"count it all joy when you fall into various trials,"* for the flesh removal in those trials is merely a part of the path toward Godly mystic development? The soul canister affirms that the believer's path is to move further and further toward Spirit, but it also shatters many of the current ways to get there.

It also exposes why a 15-year Christian evangelist with three seminary degrees, or the Christian professor of theology, or the head of an international parachurch organization may be nowhere near as mystical as the newly born-again believer with a mere four months of surrendered weakness before his Lord.

We've too often replaced knowing God with knowing about Him. We've removed Christ's essence while still attempting to live by His mandates. A house "divided against itself" cannot stand, and the world has recognized it faster than the church. Sadly, many churches across America have shelved the sanctification process for the sake of institutional and cultural success. The result is a Christian throng with character and demeanor so devoid of intended purpose that it has led to Christianity's decline in the eyes of the rest of America's populous.

THE BIG QUESTION…

The question that must be asked based on these last few pages is, "Why?" If this flesh to Spirit sanctification process is so essential in the life of the believer, then why have so many misguided, deceptive, and diversionary strategies been developed to confuse this purpose? Answering that question requires us to use the soul canister metaphor to determine why God created the sanctification process in the first place. Based on the metaphor, the answer necessitates a radical paradigm shift in thinking: The purpose of the sanctification process is to create a canister devoid of flesh and brimming over with Spirit:

Because the Holy Spirit is not merely here for you – you are also here for the Holy Spirit.

Immediately, one must ask oneself why this is so difficult to accept. At its core, the central claim is that life is not just about you, your personal desires and will. Fighting such a notion already would be a place of pride, would it not? In other words, the ultimate act of humility is recognizing life isn't about you, your plans, or your agendas, even those plans in which you enlist God's help. Jesus, the ultimate Kingdom spokesperson, was the pinnacle model of humility resonating from a Spirit-rich soul canister. In the final moments before his arrest and final crucifixion, he affirms, *"Let this cup pass from me; yet not as I will, but as You will." (Matt. 26:39 NASB)* Our mandate is "to be like Christ."

Yet 2,000 years later, best-selling Christian literature by the truckloads mines principles of scripture to help the reader get whatever he or she wants out of life. Sold-out conferences help the believer achieve personal needs and desires, be it healing, financial prosperity, freedom from addiction, or a host of other "me-first" dilemmas. Worship songs place us in the central spotlight - recognizing what God did for us and how happy we are that He did it. Though not in and of themselves wrong, these self-focused accomplishments often become the benchmarks of the Christian process.

Based on the discoveries already uncovered through this metaphor of the soul canister, it would appear we've gotten much of it backwards.

When it comes to the Mission, the Holy Spirit was given the mandate. He is the general behind the order. It is the unfinished task of the Trinity. The Holy Spirit has yet to complete His portion of the assignment, because the church has placed too little emphasis on the sanctification process necessary to grant Him access. Telling people they must run to their wildernesses does not draw big crowds. It does not sell many books. It does not pack Christian conferences.

In our ministry successes, we seem to have forced the Holy Spirit, and His agenda, to the back of the bus. The modern church is so blissfully driving toward ministry or institutional destinations it doesn't even recognize the loss of the GPS system necessary for navigation. The completion of the Spirit's agenda requires Him to have open access to Spirit-rich soul canisters, men and women who, as "vessels" of the Spirit, become megaphones for His agenda. The more deliberately we expel flesh for the sake of Holy Spirit takeover of the canister, the more the Spirit has access to our bodies: i.e. our mouths, minds, hands, and feet – through which He can unveil and advance God's Kingdom desire.

There is nothing more glorious. You can strive to become yet another musician, CEO, actor, athlete, artist, millionaire, celebrity, or any other pinnacle metric of man's accomplishment. Wouldn't you rather partner with the Artisan of the universe to accomplish an agenda that was intended since the beginning of historical time? None of us can know this agenda, or its daily necessary forms, unless we remove ourselves and allow ourselves to become more filled with Spirit than with flesh: *"When I am weak, then I am strong."* Our weakness produces His strength, carried out through the same weak vessel.

In doing so, the "god of this age" is supplanted:

"Greater is He who is in you (the Spirit) than he who is in the world (the enemy)."
1 John 4.4 NASB

The enemy of mankind knows it. The enemy's only hope is a humanity too weak to incite a rebellion and too opulent to seek effective methods of illumination.

If the church is devoid of Spiritual power, it must often find human villains to attack and conquer. Using the canister metaphor, we uncover that this method of "righteously" condemning sinners is antithetical to the Spirit's purpose. If the soul is the canister, then every person on the planet, despite one's ideological, moral, or spiritual misguiding, is still a *potential receptacle* for the Spirit. Every person has the capacity to be utilized, so the enemy cannot be those who contain soul canisters, but rather the systems, strategies, and forces that attempt to embargo the Spirit and/or decimate the canister. As the Apostle Paul affirms, our battle is not with flesh and blood, but with the principalities and powers and systems of this dark age.

HOW THEN CAN WE TELL?

Once we embrace the process of soul sanctification, how can we ensure that our increased Godly mystic reality is, in fact, genuine? Thankfully, Jesus answered that question: *"By their fruit you will recognize them."* (Matt. 7:16, NIV) As a sanctified believer's level of spiritual essence increases, and his ability to operate in various aspects of the Spirit accelerates, so too does the fruit of the Spirit evidentially increase. The outward expression of the fruit of the Spirit becomes the gauge of the internal realities of spiritual transformation.

This is where the soul canister moves from the individual to the ecclesia – the church body. It is the responsibility of those in direct relationship with the sanctifying individual to help assess and encourage the potential depth of the Spirit. In yet another aspect of humility, it often only happens through others, those able to measure your outward expressions and interpret your growth. This shatters the programmatic mindset of discipleship and affixes the true weight of responsibility on those in leadership.

Through the metaphorical power found in the "canister," we have reignited and demystified our mystic heritage, unveiled that true power is found in ultimate selflessness, and exposed a fraction of the strategies designed to embargo the Holy Spirit's agenda. I will end with two more Biblical references that adds further weight to the canister metaphor.

First, at the well in Samaria, Jesus tells the Samaritan woman he would have given her living water. Jesus, wholly filled with God's essence, was able to reach inside His canister and extract the pure vitality of the Spirit that could forever transform. We, too, in becoming like Christ, a purely-filled canister, can be used by the Spirit in a similar manner.

And finally, one of the most quoted passages in charismatic circles is God's assurance that, *"In the last days... I will pour out my Spirit on all people."* (Acts 2:17, NIV) It is interesting to note that God said He would "pour out" and not "give" his Spirit to all flesh. Pouring out would require a receptacle. Could it be that the enemy's agenda is to create as many mechanisms as possible so that as few of the "born again" as possible are capable of holding that outpouring?

In the next chapter I will give you a rather modern metaphor to greater clarify this understanding and relationship.

CHAPTER 9:

BECOMING LIKE CHRIST (IN ACTION *AND* NATURE)

The process of the growing relationship between the believer and the Spirit can be displayed through a rather unlikely source: The animated Pixar film, *Ratatouille*.

This wonderfully profound film features an inquisitive field rat named Remy. Remy, among other things, has a penchant for cooking and fine cuisine. His rat family, of course, has a hard time accepting his flair for gourmet food. After all, he's a rat. Soon, Remy and his family are forced to leave their country homestead, separated and scattered under the streets of Paris, the fine dining capital of the world. Remy's idol, a deceased chef named Gusteau, serves as a sort of spiritual guide for Remy, "providentially" directing the rat from the squalor of the sewers to the top terrace of his once famous restaurant: Gusteau's.

From that vantage point above the restaurant, Remy spies a bungling stick of a young man named Linguini. Linguini, we discover, wishes to be a cook. But as he attempts to secretly "flavor" the house soup in the kitchen, we realize very quickly – he has no cooking talent. Seeing how Linguini has botched the soup, Remy swoops into the restaurant kitchen, turning Linguini's putrid soup into a culinary delight. Remy's cookery euphoria is quickly put into perspective. Remy is captured and nearly killed because, after all, he's a rat, and rats don't belong in the kitchen.

Then something fascinating happens. The customers and the chefs in the restaurant think that Linguini is the master behind the soup. The head chef offers Linguini a position in the kitchen and gives him his first assignment: recreating the soup. Linguini, however, can't cook. The problem seems insurmountable until Remy, through a series of events, realizes he can control the movements of Linguini's body by tugging on various parts of Linguini's hair.

We then come to a scene featuring the now semi-in-sync Remy and Linguini attempting to make dinner. Testing the hair phenomenon, Remy pulls on Linguini's various hair follicles for the needed motor movements required in the kitchen. At first, it's awkward and clumsy, with Linguini/Remy knocking over bottles of wine and flipping food out the window. As they continue to work the process, Linguini/Remy begin to coalesce, their movements slowly start to become one. The last moment of the scene is Linguini/Remy working in perfect concert with each other, performing difficult culinary techniques with ease and grace.

This is perhaps the best modern day picture I can give of the desired relationship between the believer and the Spirit. As we begin to partner with the Spirit, we may be unsure of our words and our actions. Listening to the "still small voice" takes practice. Moreover, the Spirit often doesn't reveal the full picture of what to do in any particular situation. Sometimes the Spirit may only provide you with a single word to speak in a moment, but stepping out in faith on a single word or picture can reveal a myriad of information to follow. As we learn to listen, as we strive to have "ears to hear," the relationship between our will and the Spirit's agenda begins to fuse.

This is who Christ was, 100% human, and 100% God. We can say that 100% of Jesus' human will was 100% connected to God's will. Christ was our historical model of what we should become. Let me be clear, none of us can ever reach the pinnacle of Christ in nature, but we can daily strive to be like Him. The sanctification process creates this fusion. In becoming more Spirit than flesh, we further embody the nature of Christ.

CHAPTER 10:

BECOMING SPIRIT "LISTENERS"

If our focus is the Mission, and our role is the fusion of the will of the Believer with the will of the Spirit, then a considerable portion of our "walk" requires us to become Spirit "listeners." If the Holy Spirit accomplishes the Mission through us, then we must be able to discern the Kingdom words and thoughts necessary to see the Mission propagate. We need to "tune" ourselves toward the voice of the Spirit.

One of the key ways for this to happen to us is to distance ourselves from the current noise. In the scriptures, the enemy of mankind is referred to as a "roaring lion." We also see through the life of Elijah that the Spirit of God speaks to us in a still small voice. Let's look at this logically for a moment. How do you hear a still small voice over a roaring lion? If neither nature changes, it would seem nearly impossible that one could ascertain the quieter over the louder utterances. In fact, it's true. If both voices were standing next to you, it would be impossible to hear the softer voice.

The issue isn't vocal resonance; *it's proximity.*

If you are fifty feet away from the roaring lion, the power of his voice is deadened by distance, so the loudest voice in proximity is the quieter voice. Neither voice changed its nature. It was your decision to distance yourself from the louder noise.

For me, disconnection came out of a two-year media fast. At the end of 2003, I felt "impelled" to turn off television, radio and movies for what turned out to be two years. Before that moment, I was a pop-culture glutton. I reveled on the noise. I used to suck in about five hours of nightly television before my head hit the pillow. Family time with my daughter consisted of her sitting next to me while I devoured the latest role-playing game on my PlayStation 2. If I wasn't in front of the television, I was online scouring the Internet for the latest viral video. I was busy about being busy. For 10 years I had not read more than the occasional entertainment magazine clipping or a video game review online. I hadn't journaled or even considered the concept. I did everything I could to fill quiet moments with media noise, and I could finish Trivial Pursuit's Entertainment Edition in record time.

Then in November of that year, I specifically felt called to start a "media fast." That left a huge void in my schedule, so I replaced the time I had spent as a media glutton and gorged myself on literature, philosophy and Biblical teaching. I read about 70 books in those two years in addition to spending about two or three hours in daily scripture reading and meditation. I specifically spent a great deal of time in the book of Proverbs, the ultimate "word picture" book.

Very quickly, I began to hear a different voice, one that filled page upon page of journals and led me to become a writer. Since that time, I have spoken at numerous churches, conferences and seminars. I have worked with leaders in ministry and business, helping them to see the "big picture" when it comes to faith, culture, and strategic success.

Honestly, very little of that success and opportunity has come from me. It has come from listening to the Spirit of God, and allowing Him to shape my actions and my character. If we recognize it, any great author can become our mentor. We merely need to read their work and apply their principles until their words become an integral part of our lives. As we learn to listen to the Spirit and act accordingly, He not only becomes our Mentor, but we also begin to intuitively behave according to His past guidance and instruction.

Your path may be radically different than mine, but asking God to speak through His Spirit, and removing the flesh in your canister for the sake of the Mission and for the sake of Christ remains the same. Take time to reflect with God on the specific process in your life for garnering entrance into fulfilling the Mission.

CHAPTER 11:

THE GRACIOUSNESS OF THE SPIRIT

The power of this Believer/Spirit fusion isn't in its spectacle or show, but in its subtlety. You don't have to broadcast what the Spirit is instructing you to say or to act upon; you simply make it a casual part of a conversation or moment. I believe that this is a depiction of the modern day prophet. It is not the man or woman sitting in the gold-encrusted chairs on television placing their hands up to their foreheads dramatically and stating, "I have a word… " It's men and women who have decreased the flesh in their soul canisters and have asked the Spirit to fill the void, speaking in Spirit-led conversation and action throughout their entire day, usually without anyone even being aware of the moment.

68 MISSION

Remember Jesus' parable of the Sower?

> *"And He spoke many things to them in parables, saying, 'Behold, the sower went out to sow... And others (seeds) fell on the good soil and yielded a crop, some a hundredfold, some sixty, and some thirty. He who has ears, let him hear.'"*
> Matthew 13: 3, 8-9 NASB (parentheses mine)

Notice what Jesus stated! He's talking about seed that falls on "good soil." Words that, when received, have a hundred fold impact on the listener. What does Jesus say next?

"He who has ears, let him hear."

We tend to focus on this statement after this passage as a reference point to the parable: There is mystery to this parable, and so those with the right "ears" can perceive the meaning.

What if, however, verse 9 is the condition for verse 8?

What if those that can hear and then speak the words they have heard from the Spirit are those that "yield a crop, some a hundredfold, some sixty and some thirty?" If we are speaking the words of the Spirit, then they are words teeming with the Mission. Why do they create so much impact?

> *"Now there are varieties of gifts, but <u>the same Spirit</u>."*
> 1 Cor 12:4 NASB (emphasis mine)

THE GRACIOUSNESS OF THE SPIRIT

> *"But to each one is given the manifestation of the Spirit <u>for the common good</u>."*

1 Cor 12:7 NASB (emphasis mine)

Remember that the Spirit, and the Spirit's Mission, operates through born-again humanity. We are all given the same Spirit at salvation, but that Spirit requires us to manifest His agenda. In other words, when we speak words that the Spirit gives us, they are coated with Kingdom authority to accomplish the Mission. If they are coated with that authority through the speaker, then they are words that the Spirit uses in the life *of the listener* from that moment forward. I have numerous examples in my life, where I have spoken what the Spirit has instructed to me to say, and six months to years later that person will confide: "David, I've never been able to shake what you said to me."

That is the Spirit in one person connecting to the same Spirit in another person. We activate Kingdom dynamics every time we speak a Spirit-infused word, creating a network of the Kingdom, based on the words and actions spoken from us to others.

Doesn't this work in the opposite way? Haven't you been in a moment of anger or frustration and felt the tug of the enemy of mankind in your mind give you the perfect negative thought to speak out at that moment? We know if we speak that thought, especially to another person, it creates a powerful negative bond. Think about when you were little and someone called you weak, or a loser, or ugly. How long has it been since you've been able to shake those words? I know someone who was only once called an "idiot" by her father; she has yet to fully recover from those words.

70 MISSION

As life-affecting as those words may be, take heart:

"Greater is He who is in you (the Spirit), than he who is in the world (the enemy of mankind)."
I John 4:4 NASB (parentheses mine)

The reason we often don't see this "Spirit listening" reality manifested is that we have become greater listeners to the voice of the enemy rather than the voice of the Spirit. It is not necessarily our fault. From a young age, chances are that most of us were surrounded by negative thoughts and attitudes from our peers. That impact carries with us through our adult years. Becoming a Spirit listener, like Remy/Linguini, is a deliberate choice. We have to learn to "disconnect from the noise" that has plagued us for decades, so that we can hear a new Kingdom dialog. In doing so, powerful things will begin to happen…

CHAPTER 12:

THE POWER OF "SECOND BREATH"

Take a look at the following list of astounding but highly varied feats and ask yourself: What is the single requirement necessary for them all?

- Scaling the top mountain peaks of K2 or Everest
- Shallow-water diving for precious pearls on the ocean floor
- Battling victoriously in a time-extended sword fight
- Performing as an opera singer at Carnegie Hall
- Winning the Tour de France, Boston Marathon or Ironman Triathlon

At first it might appear that athleticism and physical build would be the cohesive link. Yet most opera singers are not blessed with the musculature of an Ironman Triathlete, nor could most ever hope to scale Everest. The physical requirements for climbing K2 and the athletic conditioning for sword fighting are considerably varied. Climbers are encouraged to lose weight, where overpowering size might be what tips a sword fight in a warrior's favor.

It cannot be endless years of practice, either. A mere five- or six-year-old child can be a valued pearl diver, but could never compete in the Tour de France, scale Everest, or win the Boston Marathon. There is a single collective requirement necessary for accomplishing all of these amazing escapades. It's not training. It's not athleticism. It's not muscularity or body coordination.

It's breath.

Though we marvel at athleticism and muscularity, and athletes hire strength-conditioning trainers for hundred of dollars per hour, without breath, success in these world-class events would be futile. It cannot simply be breath alone; each one of us breathes in and out at intervals of three to eight seconds all day, every day. What separates us from all those having accomplished the feats on this list, then, is *breath capacity*. How much breath, or air, your body can hold becomes the critical cohesive factor in whether you can scale mountain peaks; uncover great and priceless underwater treasures; be heralded as victorious in a critical sword battle; or receive the prize and accolades in a contest of endurance, athleticism, or vocal prowess.

THE POWER OF "SECOND BREATH"

Looking at the outcomes produced from the list above, it's easy to see how metaphorically positive and potent these actions are. You can view the world from heights only a select few ever see; live in financial prosperity and freedom through the sale of your ocean treasures; win a personal war; or achieve world-renown, acclaim, and praise. These are special, rare feats only a very few can claim to have accomplished, and they all require substantial breath capacity to achieve.

Let's get logical for a moment. If these actions all have such strong positive metaphorical and even scriptural support, such as running a race or fighting in person-to-person combat, then would not breath, as the cohesive component to them all, also be spiritually significant? To answer this, we need to understand "breath" scripturally and etymologically. We discover in Genesis that when God created man (Adam) he breathed the breath of life into him. That first natural breath gave mankind the raw resource to achieve all the natural feats cataloged at the beginning of this chapter. Then in the book of Acts, we read that the risen Christ, the new Adam, breathed on His band of uncertain and disjointed disciples to receive the Holy Spirit. The English term "breath" is the Hebrew word "ruach." The definition includes the term, "spirit." It was not just that the disciples had received the Spirit; they had received a second *spiritual* breath, as well.

Jesus said of John, the last of the prophets of natural first breath, that he was the greatest of all those having come before him. Moments later, in Matthew 11:11, Jesus declared that the least in his Kingdom, those with second spiritual breath, were greater than John. Again, Jesus told his disciples that they, only after second breath, would do greater works than even He had done. In fact, Jesus told them to wait in

Jerusalem and do nothing until they had received this second breath. The rest of the book of Acts catalogs the radical feats accomplished after His disciples received second breath. The apostles began to supernaturally heal, raise people from the dead, prophesy about future events with stunning clarity, stave off physical ailments, and lead thousands to Christ through minimal sermonettes.

Let's do a natural/supernatural comparison. Is not raising someone from the dead a far greater feat than winning the Tour de France or performing in an opera at Carnegie Hall? Would not someone prefer to be healed of cancer or AIDS than be given a necklace of black pearls and remain ill? The second breath is far greater than the first breath, because while the first breath is "human breathed," the second breath is "heaven breathed." Since first breath is "our" breath, its accomplishments are limited to our own physiologic capacity. Second breath is "His" breath. It is a form of breath with accomplishments that have no ceiling! Why? It is not tied to man's physiologic nature. It is tied to God's nature.

If first breath is the critical link between all these natural, world-renowned successes, and second breath became the conduit for all of the supernatural manifestations in the book of Acts, then why don't we hear about more supernatural phenomena occurring in our culture? Nearly every Christian denomination agrees that a believer receives second breath, the Holy Spirit, at his or her salvation. So what gives?

It may be because second breath also is about capacity.

In the physical, breathing is little more than a natural reflex. The ability to breathe doesn't qualify us to dive for treasures, accomplish great feats of battle, sing in an opera in front of thousands, or scale the heights of the Earth. Neither does the mere presence of the Holy Spirit's second breath allow us to accomplish commensurate and surpassing spiritual feats.

As reborn "second breath" Christians, we have the potential for feats greater than any feats in the natural, but our lack of breath capacity has staved off their reality. St. Irenaeus proclaimed, "The glory of God is man fully alive." Instead of being fully alive in great second breath capacity, the church, to many, appears to be somewhat on spiritual life support. What does that do for God's glory?

Too often we cry out to God for more of His glory, when He's calling out to us to become vessels able to contain what's already available.

The term "revival" often constitutes the desire for something whose dormancy lies outside of mankind, but it is man that is dormant. We don't just need revival. We need repentance. We don't just need more of Him (breath). He needs more of us (capacity). This may sound like some typical church mantra, but Jesus divulged, in exacting detail, His Father's "breath" formula.

It was the Son of God who declared:

"And no one puts new wine into old wineskins; or else the new wine will burst the wineskins and be spilled, and the wineskins will be

ruined. But new wine must be put into new wineskins, and both are preserved."
Luke 5:37-38, NKJV

Understanding that the wine in this passage is a metaphor for the Holy Spirit, or the second spiritual breath, and the wineskin is the metaphor for the heart, we can retranslate the passage above to read: "God cannot put greater second breath into a heart unable to handle its capacity. If He does, the new breath will burst the heart. No, second breath must be placed in a heart able to handle its capacity."

Is this a far stretch from Christ's intended meaning? Is there a breath/heart relation to the far superior supernatural acts those with the second breath are to achieve? To answer that question is to go back to our natural breath scenarios. Here again is the list of astounding natural feats:

- Scaling the top mountain peaks of K2 or Everest
- Shallow-water diving for precious pearls on the ocean floor
- Battling victoriously in a time-extended sword fight
- Performing as an opera singer at Carnegie Hall
- Winning the Tour de France, Boston Marathon, or Ironman Triathlon

What would happen to an individual attempting to accomplish these astounding natural feats without the proper breath (lung) capacity? Pushing the incapable body to the degree demanded by these actions would produce immense stress on the lungs. Unable to process the amount of air intake necessary, the lungs would start to collapse. The failure of the lungs would cause so much pressure that the natural heart, unable to pump fast enough to remedy the cataclysmic situation, would… burst.

> *And no one puts new wine into old wineskins; or else the new wine will burst the wineskins….*

Our God, the supernatural Creator and Author of our universe and mankind, created a physically observable metaphor that unlocks the secret to our supernatural success. He did not merely say it with His words; He proved it through His crafting of man's own physiology. God made man so that He could not accomplish humanity's most astounding natural feats without first breath capacity, just as man cannot accomplish His astounding supernatural feats without second breath capacity. He made man's heart the central conduit for both. God is exacting in every aspect of the metaphor. Through the natural, He has given us the key, and the warning, to the spiritual.

HOW THEN DO WE LIVE?

We increase breath capacity through ample time in God's word, through an understanding and application of God's ordinances beyond just their moral reasoning, through a healthy and interactive prayer and meditative life, and through an impassioned love for all of those bearing God's image. We increase breath capacity as we remove flesh from our soul canisters and invite the Spirit into the voids. We especially add breath capacity when we ask God to reshape our character.

78 MISSION

God waits on mankind's second breath capacity. He lovingly does not give us the supernatural power we cry out for, which the world desperately needs, if our hearts cannot handle it. Until we, as carriers of eternal life here on earth, build strong enough second breath capacity, the world always is going to revere and honor those with first breath capacity more than us. The astounding feats listed are truly inspiring and life altering, but we were made for supernatural feats far surpassing those on the natural list the moment we were given the spiritual breath to accomplish them.

I can do all things through Christ who (whose breath) strengthens me. Phil. 4:13, NKJV (parentheses added)

"All things" means every spiritual height, every spiritual treasure, every spiritual battle, every spiritual prize and accolade. It's not some fantastical pipe dream. It's His plan. It's a glorious part of the Mission.

What's required is capacity.

CHAPTER 13:

THE UNBREAKABLE CODE

So far in this book, we have ascertained the need and Mission of the Spirit in regards to the Kingdom. We have seen our role in its participation in becoming more like Christ in nature, not just in action. We have seen how that sanctification process opens us up to the Mission as Spirit listeners and doers.

Notice that, while dealing with ideas that many people consider too mystical or kooky, I haven't fallen into that trap. Nothing said prior has been coated in religious or hyper-spiritual language. I have merely presented ideas, grounded them with scripture and furthered their validation with various metaphors and applicable stories.

80 MISSION

I now want to strip away the kookiness from probably the most hotly contested gifts of the Spirit. I want to talk about the unbreakable code.

Winston Churchill heralded it as "The Secret Weapon that won the war." It is said to have ended the Second World War two years earlier than all accounts had predicted. It saved hundreds of thousands of lives, and denied the demagogic Nazi and Axis regimes' dominion over the European and African continent. So clandestine was this "weapon" that thirty years after the war ended, its existence still remained cloaked in silence. Then in 1976, the first whisperings of the "greatest secret of World War II after the atom bomb" began to surface. Technically, it wasn't a "weapon" at all, yet it was a vital component in every facet of the Allies' military campaigns and strategies.

What was the powerful and secret component of the success of World War II? It was the collective work of 12,000 men and women living at an estate 50 miles northwest of London. A group of military and non-military personnel comprising the nation's top mathematicians, linguists, intelligence officers, communications specialists, Chess Champions, and a soon-to-be British spy novelist named Ian Fleming. They were code breakers, and they changed the face of history.

By late 1939, Hitler's Nazi Juggernaut had begun to spread its destructive supremacy across Europe. Soon, it would seem that Hitler's Third Reich was unstoppable. Their military campaigns were powerful and effective, and German U-Boat "wolf packs" were able to sink entire

THE UNBREAKABLE CODE 81

fleets of allied ships and disappear into the darkened depths unnoticed and unhindered. A large part of their success was due to the unmatched cryptographic capabilities of the German military, for they had a communique coding system that they were convinced would never be broken. The German military had put nearly unwaivering faith in a little machine that resembled a typewriter. Eventually, it would be part of the reason for their downfall.

It was called the "enigma machine." It was built by Dr. Arthur Scherbuis, a German inventor. He originally crafted the typewriter-like box for the commercial market. His goal was to create a device that could send encrypted business transactions, such as wire transfers and confidential communiques, to ensure their privacy. By 1926, the Kriegsmarine, or German Navy, began to employ Scherbuis' box, followed shortly after by the German Army. By the time the Nazi war campaigns launched, the Enigma machine network became the central nervous system of the German communications pipeline. Nearly every railway station, front line commander, U-Boat, battleship, and military outpost was furnished with an Enigma machine. German intel could pass seamlessly and undetected from one location to the next.

The reason for this sense of security was in the detail of the machine. Each Enigma operator received five rotors, three of which would be inserted into the machine at any given time. Each rotor had 26 different settings, each corresponding with a different letter of the alphabet. On a given day, the rotors might be placed in the machine in any order, at which time each rotor was given a different setting, or starting point. Adding to the complexity was the addition of plugs with electronic circuits. Each of these plugs was connected to a different setting on the rotor, and the plug settings, ten on most machines, were also switched daily. This gave the German military the odds of their code being broken as 100 million million million (that's 29 zeros) to one.

The polish Cipher Bureau was the first to discover the machines and shortly after, a mathematician named Marian Rejewski was able to break the code of the early Enigma models. Germany, however, kept improving on the machine. In 1939, with the invasion of Poland eminent, Poland decided to share its findings with its allies, France and Britain. Unfortunately, France failed to see the danger, but Britain, under the sage leadership of Winston Churchill, had the foresight to recognize the immense importance of deciphering the enigma machine's code.

He established an intelligence bulkhead in Bletchley Park, a large estate outside of London, bringing together over 12,000 men and women to crack the mysterious code of the Enigma machine. These men and women worked tirelessly day and night, slowly and methodically studying the German's coded transmissions and determining patterns in the encrypted language. It took years before they began to whittle away at the code, but historians believe that the critical work of these men and women shortened the war by nearly two years, and may have been the deciding factor between the success or failure of the Allied Forces.

What's the point of this little history lesson?

If you want to ensure that an enemy is tactically undermined, you simply need to infiltrate their communications network.

By pilfering your enemy's communications, you have full access to their potential logistics, strategies, and tactics. You are able to plan your course of action based on ascertaining what your enemy plans to launch at you. Because of this, the military spends millions and millions of dollars on unbreakable encryption systems, and an equal amount on experts who can break the encryption systems of rival nations. By intercepting your opponent's transmissions, you render their covert tactics invalid. Decrypting your enemy's messages is a key component in keeping him on the defensive, not the offensive…

> *"In the same way, the Spirit helps us in our weakness. We do not know what we ought to pray for, but the Spirit himself intercedes for us with groans that words cannot express."*
> Rom. 8:26 NIV

> *"For one who speaks in a tongue does not speak to men but to God ; for <u>no one understands</u>, but in his spirit he speaks mysteries."*
> I Cor. 14:2 NASB (emphasis mine)

From a tactical standpoint, *speaking in tongues* is, among many other things, an impenetrable coded communication from an individual to his communications center. Unlike the Enigma and various other coding strategies that eventually were broken, it is impossible to decrypt this code. From a militaristic standpoint, this means that the enemy of mankind has absolutely no way of planning a counter attack. He is subjected to what the Bletchey code breakers referred to as continual periods of "darkness." The enemy can only suffer the outcome of the event, without ever understanding what the communication entailed and what can be done in the future to prevent it.

Consider if you will, Screwtape from C.S. Lewis' *Screwtape Letters*. As his charge prays to God over an issue of lust, crying out to God out loud, Screwtape sits with a pad and pencil transcribing all of the ways in which his charge prays and the methodology behind what got him to this moment of prayer in the first place. Soon, Screwtape has built up a rather detailed dossier of his charge, knowing when and where the weaknesses are for the next attack.

Now, suppose the person prays in tongues in the same setting. Screwtape remains mystified, as his charge speaks to God in a language he will never decipher. All of sudden, Screwtape feels a sharp slash across his chest as an angel who has been released through the clandestine prayer of his charge steps onto the scene. With a heavenly command, the angel sends Screwtape back to his lair. As Screwtape sits with his superior for a strategic debrief, his demonic commander asks him for details. "I don't know," Screwtape bemoans, "he was speaking in tongues." "Well, how do we counteract this moment?" his superior questions. "I don't know," Screwtape reasserts, "he was speaking in tongues."

We have no idea what is released into the spiritual realm as we speak to God in tongues. The Mission perpetuates and grows, without the enemy the least bit aware of what has transpired. The Mission is one of the main reasons for the war, and tongues becomes a heavenly unbreakable code, moving mountains in the Spiritual realm, without any recourse or counter strategy from the opposition.

CHAPTER 14:

INTERCESSION... WITHOUT CEASING

Intercession is another Spiritual distinction clouded in mystery. An intercessor is, in essence, a man or woman able to connect to the *will of God* in prayer, and pray His will over a situation, location or individual. While most people pray for God to answer *personal* requests and desires, an intercessor listens for God's heart in a matter, and uses his or her voice to speak out that will. For many, this is considered a gift that is given to a particular few: those with the "gift of intercession." But if we combine a couple of Biblical passages, we can see just how poignant and necessary this Spiritual ability becomes in our Mission-oriented life. Look at the verse from the previous chapter:

88 MISSION

> *"In the same way, the Spirit helps us in our weakness. We do not know what we ought to pray for, but the <u>Spirit himself intercedes</u> for us with groans that words cannot express."*
> Rom. 8:26 NIV (emphasis mine)

Let's combine it with this verse:

> "Pray without ceasing."
> I Thes. 5:17 NASB

The Bible calls us to "pray without ceasing," which, if you think about it, would be really hard to do. After all, we have to work, eat, communicate with friends, and accomplish a million other things in our day. Unless we live a monastic life, non-ceasing prayer would be difficult, but what if we looked at the verse this way:

"INTERCEDE without ceasing."

Now we have something new, and incredibly practical. Romans 8:26 states, the Spirit intercedes on our behalf, and I Thessalonians may have stated that we are called to intercede without ceasing. Then our role is to constantly live in a state of intercession, or allowing the Spirit to ubiquitously intercede through us, during any moment of our day.

Intercession becomes a life practice, not an isolated event. If intercession becomes a life-practice, then it has to assimilate *NATURALLY* into our daily events and communications. In other words, we strip the religious pretense and visual display out of

INTERCESSION… WITHOUT CEASING

intercession. Intercession without ceasing simply looks like our daily life. We continue to work, eat, communicate with friends, and accomplish a million other things in our day, all the while listening to the voice of the Spirit who knows what we are to speak and what we are to do.

In this manner, we can say that this form of intercession is the lifeblood of the Mission. Intercession becomes the distinction that sums up everything that has been spoken up to this moment in the book. It encapsulates the Spirit's agenda, unveils the symbiotic partnership we must embody, and displays how we are called to live in our daily lives.

You, for the sake of the Mission, are now an intercessor.

RESISTANCE

CHAPTER 15:

THINKING BEYOND THE "CHURCH LADY"

As wondrous as the Mission is, it has its adversaries. As we have learned there is an enemy to the Mission, the Spirit, and to us. His name in scripture is Satan. For some, even the name evokes the memory of Dana Carvey's famous *Saturday Night Live* sketch.

"Oh, who could be influencing your lusty behavior, oh who could it be... *could it be* SATAN?!"

The hyper-moral, out-of-touch woman that Carvey portrayed on SNL made a humorous mockery of a very real enemy. Therefore, I'd like to give you a new picture to wrap our heads around.

94 MISSION

For a moment I'd like you to mentally picture the one person on this planet who, like nails on a chalkboard, irritates, aggravates, or frightens you like no other person can. The individual who, at the very mention of his or her name, causes your fists to ball up, your muscles to tighten, your skin to crawl, and sadly, maybe even your eyes to tear. Perhaps it's the greasy-haired office predator with the wandering eyes; the smelly, over-the-top relative you pray skips the family reunion; the brazen, foul-mouthed shock jock that repulses you after seeing his smug face plastered on billboards; or the ex-friend that turned your afternoon chats into neighborhood gossip. Perhaps it's worse – much worse.

Think about how utterly repellent this person is, how much avoiding them for the rest of your life is one of your greatest aspirations. Ponder his or her annoying traits, the strange mannerisms, those vile facial expressions, or that arrogant and condescending smile. If you can, reflect on what he or she may have done to you to deserve this foul title. I'm sure by now you're utterly sick of having to relive this torturous mental picture, so I'll get to the point.

Now imagine that *everyone on the planet* looked just like that person.

What if there were no place to flee from that foul, anger-producing image you so wanted to erase from your memory bank? Imagine you had to endure that image, minute by minute, day by day. It's a rather horrific thought, isn't it?

This is how the enemy sees all of mankind.

For <u>everyone</u> on the planet is made in God's image. Everywhere he turns, he is faced with the image of his arch nemesis, the One whom he despises. The One he wishes to see destroyed. He can't get at his ultimate enemy: God. But he can get at that enemy's image.

Therefore, <u>everyone</u> is a target.

Like the claim of a global crime scene, we are ALL in the crosshairs, whether or not we acknowledge – or even believe – it. Connecting the dots reveals the issue is even bigger than us as Image bearers. For the staving off of the Mission is the enemy's end game. Better said, the completion of the Mission is the final end of the enemy.

While our image is a vile aggravation, our ability as Mission builders is the central focus of the enemy's firepower. In the coming pages, I will show how we, as God's image bearers and God's children, have helped the enemy to delay the Mission.

Some of what you are about to hear will be obvious to you. Some of this content may surprise you, as it has me. The more informed we become, however, the more we can counteract these powerful strategies against the Mission.

CHAPTER 16:

SARCASM – THE THICKENING

"...[D]o not harden your hearts as you did in the rebellion, during the time of testing in the wilderness...."
Heb. 3:8, NIV

This first form of resistance may seem like a benign anomaly, but when we understand how sarcasm interacts in our lives, we can see its detrimental impact on the Mission.

My wife hates sarcastic humor. To her it's equivalent to nails on a chalkboard. The instant she hears a good-natured biting joke or a humorous sarcastic comment she disconnects. The first few years of our marriage, this disconnect presented a monumental problem. The one she disconnected from the most often was her husband. I had spent more than 15 years meticulously crafting my personality around sarcastic humor, training myself in the fine art of extracting laughter out of poking fun at others. Because of this, many conversations grew instantly volatile as my "personality" got the best of me in her presence. Needless to say, since my persona was so entangled in sarcasm, there were many laugh-less nights at home.

Around almost every other human being on the planet, I was the life of the party. Laughter effortlessly flowed as I poured out my sardonic wit on those around me, but returning home, I endured nearly dry silence. Don't get me wrong; there still was conversation, but none of the gut-wrenching merriment I had concluded my soul desperately thirsted for. Finally, feeling completely dejected and a little perturbed at my wife for turning this "wild and crazy guy" in public into little more than a droll orator at home, I took the situation to God. It was a rather selfish appeal. "Oh Father," I'm sure I began, "Why do all my friends, and almost everyone I've ever come in contact with, enjoy and laugh at sarcastic but good-natured humor, and yet my wife is so perturbed by it? What is wrong with her?"

The answer sliced through my soul like a surgeon cutting away a malignant tumor without first administering anesthesia. "What's wrong with her," came back the response, "is that her heart has not grown hard enough to consider what grieves My Spirit as humorous." In a micro-moment I realized my failure, and my flaw. Based on the like-minded masses around me, I thought my wife was the abnormal one.

Instead, she was actually one of the few holdouts carrying a spiritual trait all Christians are commanded to embody.

The fact that that my wife is now such an anomaly is far more calculated than one might presuppose.

GOING GREEK

The Biblical Worldview provides some valuable insights into this condition – and its accompanying strategies. One of the Greek terms in the Bible for "harden" is "pwrovw" (pronounced "po-ro'-o). It means to cover with a thick skin or to harden by covering with a callus. Through this definition, we learn that a hardened heart is a "thick heart." Why would "thickening" be an important distinction when associated with the heart? In Matthew 9:17, Jesus states that "no one puts new wine into old wineskins." Metaphorically, Jesus is speaking of the Holy Spirit as the wine and the heart as the wineskin. Throughout the New Testament, and through the insights in this book, we discover that the Creator must change the wineskin (heart) of a "reborn" Christian so that the essential wine (the Holy Spirit) can be placed into a receptacle capable of receiving it. If the heart is the wineskin, and the Holy Spirit is the wine, what is the effect of a hardened or "thickened" heart? The thicker the heart, the less room to contain the wine.

Sarcasm is self-focused, not Spirit-focused. The purpose of sarcasm is to tear down for the sake of building oneself up. The purpose of the Spirit is to build up for the sake of new revelation and realization of the Kingdom Mission. When we are engaged in sarcasm, we are not 100% present in the conversation. Our minds are scouring what is being told to us for the sake of turning it around and skewing it for our own self-oriented, yet humorous, purposes. We *are* in the process of listening, but not to the nudging of the Spirit, but to the nudging of ourselves, or worse, to the nudging of the enemy.

The Bible claims that the enemy is bent on the wholesale destruction of mankind, not just the Christian. But Christians, those "reborn" in Christ, are the only part of mankind able to resist and threaten him and his destructive agenda. Because there is such an enemy, this thickening would be a highly advantageous strategy against the Christian.

The Bible also claims that this enemy is capable of influencing unsaved and/or prideful humanity, or what the Bible calls "the sons of disobedience". To the Christian, this enemy may manifest itself as a voice of condemnation. To the sons of disobedience he often acts as *a voice of inspiration*, contributing counsel directly into the minds of those he hates, much like a despotic dictator using captured prisoners for his own selfish benefit before their ultimate annihilation.

This is a highly advantageous opportunity. If a heart filled with the Holy Spirit is a threat to this enemy's existence, would it not be strategic to "inspire" mankind to produce self-perpetuating and engaging devices, processes and formulas that were deliberately designed to slowly thicken the heart? This way the individual rarely retains awareness of his or her heart growing continually and perpetually thicker. All the while these systems are carefully and calculatedly crowding out the space capable of holding the life-transforming and enemy-destroying "wine" of the Holy Spirit.

It's an issue of POWER.

The thickening of your heart is designed to keep you powerless. You, as a true Christian through the strength of the Holy Spirit, are one of the only ones on the planet with power over the enemy of mankind and his destructive agenda against all of humanity. The enemy knows it.

In Genesis 29, we learn of a roving vagabond of a man named Jacob who, in his journey, comes to a well used to water three flocks of sheep. Nearing the well, we learn there's a problem for the thirsty, hurried wanderer: a stone lay blocking the mouth of the water source.

> "When all the flocks were gathered there, they would then roll the stone from the mouth of the well and water the sheep, and put the stone back in its place on the mouth of the well."
> Gen. 29:3, NASB

The stone had to be removed in order for the sheep, and Joseph, to be watered. There is a vital key here. If one wanted to weaken, emaciate, or annihilate the sheep, one simply kept the stone in place. The life-giving water always was present, but destroying the health, vitality and potential of the sheep required some obstacle to hold back the life source.

If we keep adding stones, soon the water will be lost in the well.

Jack Johnson, *"Traffic In the Sky"*

In the same way, the strategy of the thickening in our lives creates a callous stone whose purpose is to prevent the watering of ourselves in the power of the Holy Spirit, and through this lack of powerful spiritual nourishment, the rest of the sheep – or mankind universal.

Let me offer one more example to further unpack this revelation. If you have any inkling towards evangelism, chances are you have quoted the passage in Revelation, *"Behold, I stand at the door and knock. If anyone hears My voice and opens the door, I will come in to him and dine with him, and he with Me."* (Rev. 3:20 NASB) It is often used to describe a preconversion nudging of God. God knocks, waiting for the man or woman to open his or her heart to Him and grant Him that wondrous access, but the Greek terms used in this verse are in the continual present tense. We could say it this way: "Behold, I am constantly standing at the door and knocking, if anyone keeps hearing my voice and opens the door, I will constantly come in to him and keep dining with him, and he with Me." This "knocking" is not just the moment of salvation, but a continual dialog Jesus is offering the believer. If God is constantly knocking on the mind of the believer, then what is the enemy's strategy?

Thicken the door.

Have you ever come up to a home or building with a thick wooden door? Consciously or not, we rap harder on the door. There is more depth to the wood and more force must be utilized to ensure those on the other side hear our knocking request. Jesus is always knocking, even speaking, on the other side, but the thicker the door, the harder it is to hear the sound. Unlike us, Jesus, most often, doesn't rap harder. Jesus is a gentleman. As C.S. Lewis stated in *The Screwtape Letters*, while the enemy "forces," God, most frequently, "woos."

By eliminating sarcasm from our lives, we shave layers off of that door, and we hollow out the callousness of our hearts. In so doing, we can begin to hear the voice of God with greater clarity.

The attitude of a person on Mission is to always encourage, strengthen, inspire and challenge those around him or her. This is difficult in the age of harsh critique and callous statements brought on by social media and digital anonymity. Still, a person on Mission constantly strives to be intentional, knowing that a single word spoken in Kingdom power can set the course of that person's life from that moment forward.

The "reward" of sarcasm lasts mere micro-moments, but the reward of Kingdom-based encouragement and inspiration can last a lifetime and, hopefully, even longer.

CHAPTER 17:

FOCUSING ON SPIRIT "PHENOMENA"

This is a sad chapter to write, because for the next couple of pages, I will show how the Mission of the Holy Spirit is being staved off by the very people who accepted His wonder. We are aware that for many denominations in Christendom, the Holy Spirit is the red-headed step child of the Trinity. He is rarely discussed, studied, or often even welcomed.

At a church in Kentucky, I heard an entire sermon from a Baptist preacher centered on the verse, *"Do not be drunk with wine, but be filled with the Holy Spirit."* He then went on to describe the phenomena of the Holy Spirit in the same negative terms as drunkenness.

At a leadership retreat at another church, the head pastor was discussing some of the hardships that his leadership team would soon face.

"Some of the people in your new small groups," he began, "will have gone through tragic circumstances in their lives. Some will have been or are still alcoholics, some will suffer from drug addiction, others have been sexually assaulted and others have spoken in tongues."

I think that Paul, the apostle, would have a hard time equating drug addiction with speaking in tongues, but this pastor's statement reflects how many in the church view the phenomena of the third part of the Trinity.

Sadly, they have their reasons.

When it comes to Spirit, a large portion of the church tends to predominantly focus on phenomena. Congregants and congregations search for the next 'move of the Spirit," often traveling from conference to conference and from spiritual leader to spiritual leader, anxiously awaiting the next "filling." Let me be clear, unlike many denominations, I fully believe in the manifestations of the Spirit. Having grown up in a charismatic church, with an Assemblies of God pastor for a father, I have seen the Spirit move in powerful ways, such as healings, prophecy, and words of knowledge.

I have also seen people wholly seek after these things rather than recognize their use in the Mission. They are content to leave the world in its current state, spending their time, talent and treasure filling up on Holy Spirit manifestations. Surprisingly, many of these people tend to be even more bitter, jealous, elitist, and unempathetic than those that don't claim to have been "filled" with the Spirit. They often speak in their own "spiritual-ish" dialect, and frequently have trouble communicating with those outside of their particular sphere of spiritual influence or denominational strain.

How is this possible?

I believe that the Soul Canister metaphor reveals part of this insight. Those who seek the phenomena of the Spirit often tend to focus on immersing the OUTSIDE of the canister, rather than replacing the fleshly contents on the inside. I believe that if the inside of the canister isn't sanctified, eventually the enemy is granted access into the phenomenological game. Remember that the Magicians in Egypt could accomplish similar phenomenological feats as Moses? The woman in Acts had the ability to prophecy over others without using the Spirit of God?

For the sake of the Mission, the question we need to be asking ourselves is not: "Am I feeling God in this phenomenological moment?" Instead, we need to inquire, "Have I removed the things in my life that could prevent this moment from being fully genuine?" Remember, Jesus again stated: *"By their fruit you will know them."* Any moment of phenomena in the Spirit needs to be immediately conditioned on the fruit of the Spirit.

108 MISSION

> *But the fruit of the Spirit is love, joy, peace, patience, kindness, goodness, faithfulness, gentleness, self-control; against such things there is no law."*
> Gal. 5:22-23 NASB

Anyone who can go from experiencing a phenomenological moment in the Church sanctuary to yelling at a worker in the children's department needs to seriously question whether the previous moment was fully genuine. It matters not whether we claim to be powerful in the phenomena of the Spirit; we must be humble men and women who consistently bear fruit in our lives and in the lives of others. Then we can be certain that the phenomena we are experiencing is both real, and Mission-minded.

CHAPTER 18:

(SELF) "RIGHTEOUS" ANGER

Another stumbling block to the Mission is (self) "righteous" anger. If you're old enough, you'll remember the lyrics to this song from one of the fathers of Christian Rock, Petra:

"We are strangers, we are aliens, we are not of this world."

When we are born again, we experience a transformation. We undergo a spiritual reshaping, where the things that used to occupy our minds and bodies no longer have the same impact and control over our lives. We do begin to hate what God hates and love what God loves, as the Spirit of God begins to reshape our thoughts, actions and, hopefully, our character.

How we express those new thoughts and intuitions either propagates or strangles the Mission. How? After all, if we are speaking truth, aren't we accomplishing God's will? Surprisingly, even if we speak complete truth, if it's spoken in the wrong way, we can destroy the very intent of the truth itself. Remember, we are to:

"... speak the truth in Love." Ephesians 4:15 NLT

The opposite goes by the term - *polarization.*

It matters not whether you are speaking complete truth or a gross fallacy. If it causes polarization, you are operating in the enemy's camp. Polarization is not a biblical concept; It is a demonic strategy. The enemy of mankind knows that if he can separate and segment various factors of society and pit them against each other, he can stave off the Mission. Remember, we are all made in the image of God. As soon as we act against that reality and, in (self) "righteous" anger, attack others made in that image, we lengthen the Spirit's assignment and we stifle the Mission.

Today, especially in America, our polarizing line is nearly at 50/50, with half of the country in opposition with the other half. While it is perfectly fine to have our own convictions, we need to be careful how we present those beliefs and morals. Again, no matter what we say, or how grounded Biblically our words may be, the outcome of the conversation must be coated in the following "fruit:"

> *"But the fruit of the Spirit is love, joy, peace, forbearance, kindness, goodness, faithfulness, gentleness and self-control. Against such things there is no law."*
> Gal. 5: 22-23 NIV

We tend to think that this means we are to exude these traits in our actions, but I believe that these fruits are also *based on outcomes*. The fruit on any tree is not an action. It is the outcome of a process. In the same manner, whatever we speak and however we act, must produce outcomes that align with the fruit of the Spirit.

In so doing, we shelve the strategy of polarization and further the Mission:

> *"Since we live <u>by the Spirit</u>, let us keep in step with the Spirit. Let us not become conceited, <u>provoking</u> and envying each other."*
> Gal 5: 25-26 NIV (emphasis mine)

We also tend to think that the more Biblical knowledge we have, the more we should speak up against those things that are antithetical to God. Since I can quote chapter and verse, I have more firepower and more authority to go after those opposing my belief system, or speaking and/or acting in error. The exact opposite may be true.

For years, the knives in my kitchen cupboard were incredibly dull. Because they were dull, whenever I cut a tomato, cucumber or whatever food item was on the chopping block, I had to exert quite a bit of force to slice through it. Then my father in law came to town. An avid knife expert and proficient marksman, he immediately went into my cupboard and started sharping my knives to razor precision.

The next time I grabbed a knife, it was a micro-moment until I realized, "Wow, this blade is sharp!" I suddenly understood that if I were to use this newly sharpened blade, I would have to be careful. The blade's new precision could hurt me, and others. Seconds later, I felt inspired that this was an example of how we need to act as we mature in our knowledge of the Word and God's ways.

Remember, the Bible is referenced as a two-edged sword. The sharper the sword, the less we need to apply force. We simply let the power of the Word do its job. Trust the wisest man who ever lived.

> *"If the axe is dull and he does not sharpen its edge, then he must exert more strength. Wisdom has the advantage of giving success."*
> Ecc. 10:10 NASB

Wisdom recognizes that the power does not come in *our* words, but in *His* words. We utilize both scripture, and the Spirit's leading, in gracious ways so that the listener receives no "offense" from us. Our words should convict, challenge, and inspire directly to the person's soul, or, if they are a believer, to the Spirit inside of them.

CHAPTER 19:

THE BODY BATTLE:

I have seen something very interesting occur at the moment a person first experiences the Spirit through speaking in tongues. At first I didn't recognize what I was witnessing, but as I watched this happen repeatedly, I gleaned a pattern to the moment.

More often that not, when a person was about to experience the gift of tounges through the Spirit, there would be a visible internal struggle. Though the person wanted the moment to occur, it simply wouldn't happen for periods of five, ten, even thirty minutes or more. It seemed to be right at their throat, but no words would come out. Then, all of sudden, there would be a breakthrough, and new Spiritual words and sounds would flow for minutes, even hours. Usually in those moments, tears would stream as quickly as the spiritual language they were now voicing.

As I watched this happen over repeated months and years, I realized that there was more occurring in that moment than just a spiritual battle. It was not simply God defeating a losing supernatural enemy.

It was a battle of the independent physical body trying to retain control of the individual's will.

Remember how Paul stated that a war existed "between his members?"

"But I see another law in my members, warring against the law of my mind, and bringing me into captivity to the law of sin which is in my members"
Romans 7:23 KJV

We tend to think of this as a volitional war. I want what I want, and God wants what He wants from me, and the tension in between His will and my will is where we live every day.

What if that war is also occurring *independently* of you and your will?

Consider, if you will, that you happened to cut yourself on a piece of glass. From the moment your body begins losing blood, the cells in your body began to collect around that wound and "clot" in an effort to stop the blood loss. Did you **will** that to happen? No, in that moment your independent body shows its true colors.

When a person falls into nearly freezing water, rescuers realize they only have micro minutes to retrieve the individual from the frigid cold, not simply because hypothermia sets in quickly, but because of what the independent body does in that moment to survive. Whenever the body experiences that kind of dramatic decrease in temperature, the body realizes that death is eminent and so it protects the central component of a functioning body, the heart. Immediately, the body begins to draw all the blood in the individual back to the central region around the heart, to keep the heart pumping. In relocating the blood to the heart, the extremities, in this case the hands and feet, no longer function at capacity, and the person, despite their will to flail and stay afloat, becomes a human sinker weight.

Although you may not be fully aware of it, your body is, in essence, its own entity. As you give in to the urges of your body, your body exerts more and more control over your will. Pleasure, pride, greed, and lust, for example, don't just feel good to you; they feel great to your independent body. But the body is not simply focused on its selfish and independent desires holistically; the entire body operates *independent* of its other members. Each organ and facet of the body is selfishly independent of the other members.

For example, my brain and my taste buds crave fatty, greasy foods. Should I give in to these urges too often, my body begins to control my thoughts and body mechanics, stimulating me toward further stepping into gluttony. Yet my heart and other organs can't handle the increase in food intake. My skin and soft tissue layers begin to suffer on account of what my brain and taste buds desire as well. What my taste buds and pleasure center in my brain continually desire wracks havoc on the rest of my independent body, even leading to the death of the entire physiological system.

The body not only works against you – it also works against itself. That moment prior to tongues, your independent body realizes it is about to lose control over your will. The person's desires are no longer centered on the desires of the body, but on the desires of the Spirit. It is one of the instrumental moments of the Mission. Your body knows it. So did Paul:

> *"but I discipline <u>my body</u> <u>and make it my slave</u>, so that, after I have preached to others, I myself will not be disqualified."*
> 1 Cor. 9:27 NASB (emphasis mine)

We can use this new understanding to expose the work of the enemy of mankind. The enemy has carefully and meticulously "inspired" humanity to adopt and sanction actions and technologies that allow the body to control the will of the individual. Many of these actions, such as drug usage, pornography, gambling, drunkenness, etc., create addictive tendencies. Many of these technologies, through technological improvement, exacerbate the addiction process. Again, this addiction doesn't just occur in the person, it occurs in and through the independent body. Science is daily uncovering how these addictive behaviors and substances affect the body through the brain.

We can say it this way: Addiction is the moment that the will of the person becomes completely dominated by the body of the person.

We now live in a culture where millions of individuals have lost the body/will battle, and are suffering in countless ways under these strategies. Shifting our mindset, sin is predominantly not about the pleasure of action, but the destruction from <u>consequence</u>. Sin's goal is death, whether that is final mortality or the death of a marriage, the death of brain cells, the death of finances, etc. Sin needs a mechanism for its intended destruction. That mechanism is most often pleasure and self based living. As we commit "sinful" actions without considering the cost, we suffer sin's *intended outcomes* in our minds, bodies, families, and societies. As those born-again, we need to become more astute at recognizing and exposing the strategies of sin, not merely attacking the "sinful" actions of humanity.

Metaphorically, sin is shards of glass coated in chocolate, which taste wonderful in the mouth and then lacerate the organs on the way down. The typical response from the church is to attack people for eating the chocolate because God "said not to." While the world sucks at the sweet coating and scoffs, "you're missing out of some of life's finest delicacies." What the church should be saying is, "Of course it's chocolate. You would never have swallowed the glass shards without it."

The Spirit's desire is to keep the individual in optimal body health because He is able to accomplish the Mission for the greatest amount of time and energy in a vessel able to function in prime health. The enemy attempts to use the body as a master over the will so that the individual is never able, or is gelded from assisting in the Mission.

CHAPTER 20:

THE "STRATEGY" OF SIN

Let's continue to talk about "sin" for a moment. Did you know that the word "sin" is actually based on a term *in archery*?

Naturally, there are four things necessary in archery, an archer, a bow, an arrow, and a target. On that target are usually painted concentric rings with a "bull's eye" in the center, and then other rings that stretch out beyond its center. The archer then stands at a distance and shoots his arrow at the target. The bull's eye is considered the place of perfect placement for the arrow. Should the archer hit the bull's eye, it is considered the "perfect" shot. Do you know what the *distance* between any shot that doesn't hit the bull's eye, or the arrow's "perfect" placement, is called?

THE "STRATEGY" OF SIN

The Sin line.

Sin is the distance between the perfect and whatever action, thought, idea, etc. we commit. The question that now arises is what is the "perfect" that God is describing when he references "sin"? Before we answer that, let us all realize that none of us can be "perfect," as God himself states:

"for all have sinned and fall short of the glory of God"
Romans 3:23 NIV

We don't need to figure out what "perfect" is; we simply need to understand what is meant by the phrase: "the glory of God." The Bible is not clear on this statement, but I believe one man created a definition that may be part of what God is defining, and it ties into the realities presented in this book. The author of the quote was a man named St. Irraneus. He was a theologian that lived in the second century. Sadly, you may not know of this man, but his declaration should have been as impactful and powerful in our historical culture as was Descartes' quote, "I think, therefore I am." Here it is...

"The glory of God is man *fully alive*."

As we have already seen, God has always desired the very best for His creation since its fall. Sin, among other things, becomes the distance man travels away from that desire. This distance isn't just personal. It can be ideological, societal, and certainly spiritual.

THE "STRATEGY" OF SIN

Sin grieves God not just because it separates us from Him, but it separates us from all He has designed us to be. Sin gives through pleasure in order to steal man's "fully alive" intention... through consequence.

Sin gelds us from participation in the Mission in two predominant ways. First, sin most often stagnates our desire to decrease the flesh in our soul canisters. If flesh and Spirit are the two forces with access to our soul canisters, then sin partners with the flesh and starves out the Spirit. Condemnation often becomes the loudest voice we hear Spiritually.

Let's look at sin scientifically.

When we commit any action through our will, we build up synaptic pathways in our brain corresponding to those actions. I believe that there is a Spiritual/Neurological connection. The paths we build in our brains give either the Spirit or the enemy of mankind authority and access in our lives.

> "In the (neurological) paths of the wicked are snares and pitfalls, but those who would preserve their life stay far from them."
> Proverbs 22:5 NIV (parenthesis added)

Until we starve those "sinful" paths, we can be subject to the louder voice of the enemy, or worse. Note what James said:

> "Therefore Submit to God, resist the devil, and he will flee from you."
> James 4:7 NKJV

Neurologically, this makes complete sense. We strengthen our "sinful" synaptic paths every time we consider those actions, such as through fantasy, or act again in a similar "sinful" manner. Even if we cry out against our "sinful" actions in prayer, we still may function along that original pathway. It is only by deliberately choosing a different course of action, which is a part of 'repentance', that we build a new pathway, and in so doing, we starve off the original sinful pathway that granted access to the enemy of mankind.

Second, when we give in to sin, we suffer sin's intended consequences in our bodies, minds, families, friendships, and societies. That consequence often becomes the *dominant focus of our wills*. You are in control of your will most of your life, until, let's say, you get the flu. At that time, your body dominates your will. That's why we bury ourselves in flannel sheets and down triple shots of NyQuil. We may want to head to the ballgame, but our independent body has a different desire. In the same manner, once we suffer the intended outcomes of sin in our bodies and minds, and not just our souls, our will becomes a greater slave to the effects of those outcomes.

Let's suppose we can peer into the life of a man named John. John fancies himself as a bit of a 'player,' haughtily bragging to his bros', "I can sleep with whomever I want without it affecting me." In fact, that is true. He can.

Until he contracts a sexually-transmitted disease.

John now suffers from a case of Gonorrhoea H041, and the domination over his will begins to escalate. First, there's the pain in his body. That quickly affects his mental ability, which is now heavily preoccupied. John also faces the shame of knowing that he's now a "marked" man, and his relational life will forever suffer. He also has to visit the local clinic two times a week after contracting the disease to assess its spread and manage symptoms.

The problem is that visiting the clinic requires him to leave the office during the 9 to 5 workday. Let's suppose John was the top salesperson in the company, and because of his new absences and his new mental state, John loses the company's top client, or 20% of the organization's yearly profits.

Because of the loss in revenue, the company fires two of its lower tier employees. That puts one of the fired employee's son's college tuition in jeopardy, and he must attend a lower grade college, stifling his financial future after he leaves the less prestigious school. The other fired employee suffers more than just financial and psychological recourse. That employee had a seven-dollar-a-day latte habit at Starbucks. Unable to visit "the 'bucks" anymore, Starbucks loses $1,820 per year, and because of some other financial hits, they let one of their baristas go, causing another chain reaction.

The rabbit hole could have gone so much deeper. I just chose to end it there for the sake of brevity. This is one of the main strategies of sin. It is not about the initial action, but the myriad of future caustic and debilitating *consequences*. In each case, each individual loses control of some portion of their will, and in so doing, unwittingly focuses on

124 THE "STRATEGY" OF SIN

that area of domination instead of being led by the Spirit and furthering the Mission.

ON MISSION

CHAPTER 21:

LEARNING TO LIVE "ON MISSION"

You have now seen examples of the resistance to the Mission. It's time to reveal some of the traits of living "on Mission." This is in no way an exhaustive list, but instead are principles and character traits that I feel are necessary to live a Mission-oriented, Kingdom-centered, Spirit-rich, lifestyle.

By learning to become more intentional in your thoughts, words, and character, you are given access to the Mission in ways that others may not experience. Remember Jesus' repeated assurance:

"He who has ears to hear, let them hear."
Mark 4:9 NASB

LEARNING TO LIVE "ON MISSION"

And God's declaration in 2 Chronicles:

> "For the eyes of the LORD move to and fro throughout the earth that He may strongly support those whose heart is completely His."
> 2 Chronicles 16:9 NASB

My hope is that these "on Mission" points will help you condition your ears and focus your eyes for the greatest amount of Spirit-fused reception.

For when you are living "on Mission," you no longer need to strive. You don't need to worry if you are being effective. Striving and worry are a result of <u>uncertainty</u>. As we speak the words of the Spirit, and act according to His desires, we remain confident that our words and actions have spiritual power and authority to carry out the Mission. We are then certain through the FRUIT that outflows from those words and actions.

While we are becoming Spirit Listeners and doers, we also must daily live in excellence in *everything* we do. Chances are, we will not hear the Spirit at all points in the day, but as we strive to excel in all aspects of our lives, we can be certain that we are living on Mission. Proverbs assures:

> "Do you see a man skilled in his work? He will stand before kings; He will not stand before obscure men."
> Proverbs 22:29 NASB

We must live, work, and play in excellence, all the while continuing to listen intently to the voice of the Spirit for Mission-infused moments. Perhaps the best description of this relationship between a life lived in excellence and a prayerful, Spirit-rich relationship follows below. I've changed a few words for effect.

"Get on your knees and pray, then get off your butt and work."

When we are off Mission, we tend to focus on either opposite:

Either we spend our time in prayer and Spiritual things, and become lazy in our daily responsibilities.

Or, we focus all of our intention on striving and success and our spiritual life is placed on the back burner.

Being on Mission is a balance of both arenas.

This pithy statement about "work" isn't just a vocational request: Work on your marriage. Work on your friendships. Work on your education. Work on your skillsets. Work on your character. Work on your Spiritual disciplines. Being on Mission means we are constantly growing, constantly improving, constantly falling at the foot of the cross and getting back up even stronger.

With that said, here are some of the traits and character profiles of men and women "on Mission."

CHAPTER 22:

ON MISSION: EMPATHY

A person on Mission is empathetic:

If there is one trait that the church is grossly lacking, it's empathy. The church is sympathetic at best. This is because we often fail to see that everyone, regardless of Spiritual status, is made in God's image. They may not all be God's children, but all people still bear His glorious image. We have to recognize that the enemy of mankind wishes to strip everyone of their "image of God" heritage. Unfortunately, the church tends to partner with him in letting that happen.

Here is an important frame of reference: a person's ideology, religion, sexual preference, or moral standards do not determine his or her identity; they merely help to shape his or her actions. Those actions produce *outcomes* that affect the individual and the culture at large, either positively or negatively, as I showed in the fictional story of John. Actions are subjective: I can *do* anything I want. Outcomes, however, are objective and undetermined: I don't control what happens to me, or others, after that action has been committed.

The world is rife with people who have assumed that their subjective actions wouldn't lead to caustic, uncontrollable outcomes. Now man is suffering from disease, divorce, depression, despair, ad infinitum because of the consequence of his subjective actions. Those outcomes weigh heavily on society, both individually and collectively. They have strangled humanity of God's intent: The Kingdom realized "on Earth as it is in heaven."

For the sake of the Mission, we need to lovingly address the damaging outcomes, not vehemently attack the actions propagated by those made in God's image.

We fail to realize that whenever we are standing in front of a person, the person they are – in that moment – has been shaped by decades of the enemy's attacks. Some of that attack they have given into, some has happened to them without volitional desire or ability for recourse. Others, because of what has been done or said to them in the past, have given into "ungodly" actions to deaden or distract from the pain of past hurts and abuses.

Empathy takes all this into account. It doesn't judge in the moment; it loves the person through their past and offers a better hope for their future.

We also tend to forget that prior to becoming saved, we were the very people we are now attacking. Just as we would have responded negatively to the words of those born again in our past lives, we need to empathetically understand how they perceive our words of condemnation and rebuke. Jesus embodied empathy; the Pharisees, at best, practiced sympathy. Which one was more on Mission?

CHAPTER 23:

ON MISSION: NOT KOOKY

A person on Mission isn't Kooky:
We've gone over this already, but it deserves to be readdressed. Those who appear to have been given the gift of prophecy or other gifts of the Spirit tend to use it in a manner than can be… just plain weird. A number of years ago, I was at a church where one of the pastors was praying "prophetically" over the group gathered. As she spoke, she jerked her body and blurted out various words with more force than others. One of the men in the congregation sitting next to me, a new believer, leaned over to me as she spoke. "How sad," he whispered, "she must have Turretts."

136 ON MISSION: NOT KOOKY

Many people are turned off by Christian television programming, not only because of the content of the message but also because of the way they speak. Ask yourself a question: did you ever speak like that prior to becoming saved? We often put on this new, and I would say somewhat kooky, way of speaking, that doesn't resonate with the rest of culture, By doing so, our impact and influence usually centers around those that believe in a similar manner. The bottom line is that we often fail to relate, so we retreat back to our own Christian enclave.

A person on Mission doesn't need theatrics. He or she doesn't need to speak with a "religious" tonality. He or she recognizes that the power of his or her words or actions are *already* coated with Spiritual authority. A person on Mission recognizes that the more he or she can speak like the culture in tone and delivery, the greater the Spiritual influence he or she can have across cultural, political, and religious divides.

CHAPTER 24:

ON MISSION: LISTEN MORE, TALK LESS

A person on Mission listens more than he or she talks:
Years ago, I was in a high-level business course in California. At a particular point in the course, we were studying a book entitled *The Tree of Knowledge*, by Humberto R. Maturana and Francisco Varela. This book was hyper-complex, dealing with concepts such as "ontogenic structural-pair coupling" and other confusing distinctions. Since I didn't understand what the book was presenting, I decided to put into practice what I didn't comprehend. Soon I became one of the class experts on the book.

In a study session at one of the conferences, I shared for a good fifteen of the thirty minutes of the session about my discoveries from the book. Many of the people sitting in that session, some twice and three times my young age of 25, were amazed at what I had discovered through the book. I was feeling pretty good about myself after that moment. Then my coach, who had been sitting behind me during the session, met me at the snack table.

"Wow," she said, "You sure had a lot to say during that session." "Yeah," I answered back, still feeling pretty euphoric at my shared insights. "And every one in the group got a lot out of your knowledge of the book," she mused, reeling me in. "Yeah, you're right," I considered, not realizing the sharp left turn the conversation was soon to take. "Just one question," she said with Columbo-like precision, "What did *you* get out of the conversation?"

"Excuse me?" I said, not ready for the inquiry. "Well, you took over half the time helping others. I'm just curious what you got out of listening to their advice and their knowledge of the book," she said, graciously digging the knife into my obliviousness. That moment has stuck with me for nearly twenty years. As a Spirit Listener, we need to give the Spirit moments of activation based on the dialog of others. When we are the central focus of the conversation, it is difficult for the Spirit to speak to us.

More often that not, we, like that moment I had in the study session, speak out of pride or insecurity. We like to be recognized for our insights, our personality, or our past exploits. We have to learn to put that aside, for the reward is far greater when we speak less and listen more.

I often tell others there are two ways to be recognized as the most powerful person in a room. The first way is to speak in such a commanding and lofty manner that everyone in the room bows to your intellect and alpha-like personality. The other way is to encourage, inspire, and challenge every one in the room in such a manner that they leave the room more powerful than they were when they entered.

While the first way may be more self-gratifying and ego stroking, it is also limiting and fleeting. As soon as you are brought down by someone more powerful than you, you are left reeling in your damaged pride. The Bible says:

> *"When someone invites you to a wedding feast, do not take the place of honor, for a person more distinguished than you may have been invited. If so, the host who invited both of you will come and say to you, 'Give this person your seat.' Then, humiliated, you will have to take the least important place."*
> Luke 14:8-10 NIV

Building others up is not immediately as self-gratifying. In fact, many times the people in the room rarely give you credit. In time, the reward is so much greater when you inspire others. You have the opportunity to sit back and watch those you inspire grow in wisdom and strength and know that you, through the Spirit of God, were part of making it happen.

I have often had someone share with me a powerful statement or thought that "someone" had told them in the past, often stating these words changed his or her life. Unbeknownst to them, and I certainly don't speak up, I was the one who had originally given them that thought. When we are on Mission, we don't care about taking credit. It wasn't really my insight in the first place. It was the Spirit's, acting on Mission.

CHAPTER 25:

ON MISSION: PRE-FALL EVANGELISM

A person on Mission most often takes a pre-fall approach to evangelism.

Remember how I spoke on the Kingdom and God's intent for the Earth and humanity in Chapter 4? Because we fail to understand the nature and desire of the Kingdom, we most often evangelize from a *post-fall* frame of reference. Our Gospel message usually starts at Genesis 3, not Genesis 1.

Let me show you what I mean. A common evangelistic approach usually is presented in somewhat of the following manner. From birth, you were born into a world of sin and death. Because of the sins of Adam, you have been separated from God. You live disconnected from your Creator and are destined for hell. Sin has blocked you from God. In fact, you have committed sins that have separated you from God. There is nothing you can do on your own to atone for those sins, but Jesus Christ came and died for your sins, sacrificing Himself on the cross as the atonement for sin. His death paid the way for you to receive eternal life, and you need to accept this free gift so that you can experience the joy of connecting with God and other believers and then when you die you will be with God and Christ in Heaven.

This was often the message I heard growing up. Many of my fellow classmates and Sunday school attendees were saved because of messages like this. There is nothing wrong with this depiction; it just isn't the full story. This message starts at Genesis 3, with the fall of man and the entrance of sin and judgment into the world.

The gospel, however, starts at Genesis 1, with goodness, beauty, and God's original design and intent. Therefore, we can present the gospel this way:

We were created in wonder, beauty, and perfection to be connected with our Creator in perfect harmony. He designed the world around us to be in concert with us, giving us every good thing because He loves us.

Then humanity, in its pride and fear, was tricked into rejecting that connection, and God's perfect desire, by the true enemy, Satan. Satan intentionally severed that connection, and attempted to strip away the wonder, beauty, and perfection that God intended for you to receive.

The enemy tricked man into inviting sin, disease and destruction into the world, and separated you from God's intention for you. God still "loves the world" and humanity, so He sent His Son to provide a bridge back to reconnection with Him through Christ's death on the cross.

Accepting Him brings you back to the desire He has always had for you: intimacy, beauty and love for His greatest creation, mankind. Accepting this free gift, your Mission becomes to spread that Gospel, the good news to others, while fulfilling the Lord's prayer of: *"Thy Kingdom come, thy will be done, on Earth as it is in Heaven."* Then, after your final breath, you will come into complete and wondrous connection with your Creator, Savior, and Lord, to live eternally with Him.

The point is, you matter! You have tremendous worth! You are incredibly special to the God that created you. He wants to regain that intimacy, connection, and beauty that He once had with humanity!

The power in this form of evangelism isn't in its presentation, but in its resonance. Remember that we are *all* made in the image of God? That image is inherent. Something deep down in us still recognizes that we were created as pre-fall beings. Something in us understands that we matter.

I have seen this happen over and over again: it doesn't matter what a person has gone through in his or her life (all post-fall circumstances), when they are addressed from a pre-fall approach, something inside of him or her resonates with the message. It's a call to the Kingdom. It creates Spirit activation, and it cuts through the lies and schemes of the enemy of mankind.

A pre-fall mindset is grounded in empathy, compassion, and love. We are all on the same playing field; we *all* were created to matter. Post-fall evangelism says, however unintentionally, that you don't matter as much as I do yet, because you haven't bridged the gap between sin and death. You are still under judgment and I am not. Let's look at a chart that revels the differences between these two forms of evangelism.

(postfall: Gospel starting with Genesis 3) **DAMAGE OF SIN.**	(prefall: Gospel starting at Gen 1:1) **GOODNESS OF THE GARDEN:**
Judgment	Love
Sympathy	Empathy (compassion)
Insider/Outsider	Collective
Goodness Corrupted by sin	Sin Corrupted that which is good!
Morality	Concern for humanity
Failure	Inspiration
Pray against the wicked people in our nation. (Outside of God's Holy Standard)	Pray for the EFFECTS of wickedness on the PEOPLE of this nation. (Outside of God's Holy and wondrous INTENT)

This is not to say that post-fall evangelism hasn't worked. It simply hasn't produced the cultural transformation that should accompany the gospel. It hasn't *"turned the world upside down."* Neither does it present the full gospel message. Apparently, those first two chapters of the Bible make a world, or better yet, a Kingdom of difference.

CHAPTER 26:

ON MISSION: RELATIONSHIP MOMENTUM

A Person on Mission furthers Relationship Momentum for the sake of the Kingdom:

A number of years ago, I put up the following facebook post:

"Today you may just be the stepping stone in someone else's destiny."

A person on Mission recognizes that if the Spirit is active in his or her life and wishes to connect to the Spirit in others, then he or she recognizes that he or she must become a relational "connector." The

Spirit doesn't accomplish the Mission strictly through our dialog or our actions.

He also manifests the Mission through *relationships*.

A good friend of mine recently wrote a book entitled *Relationship Momentum: The Secret to Making Ideas Move*. In the book, he asserts that any idea, product, government, etc., does not come together through finances, marketing, or a hefty amount of preplanning. They come together through relationships. His book is a brilliant step-by-step guide on the art and science behind building ideas, etc., through effective relationships. Based on the Mission, we could retitle his book in the following manner:

Relationship Momentum: The Spirit's Secret to furthering the Kingdom.

A person on Mission does whatever he or she can to help further the relational development of others. If they meet a struggling musician, for example, a person on Mission scours his or her smart phone contact list for the right connection in the music industry to further that person's God-ordained calling. A person on Mission finds a person in their church body with a particular skill and sets them up with others in need of that service. A person on Mission listens to the dreams of others and then finds relationships that can make those dreams happen.

ON MISSION: RELATIONSHIP MOMENTUM

A person on Mission is integral in the Providential passages of Proverbs 16, specifically Proverbs 16:9, *"In his heart a man plans his course, but the Lord establishes his steps." (NIV)* He or she recognizes that the Spirit of God is constantly building the Kingdom through *relationships*.

Sadly, many people, filled with pride and self-intention, miss their divine opportunity to be used by the Spirit in this manner. For the sake of their own agendas, they lengthen the completion of the Kingdom Mission. There have been moments in my life where I have discerned that people I am in relationship with could be integral in furthering God's plan for my life. Yet, I watch silently as they miss the opportunity to make it happen, content to satisfy their own agendas rather than use their influence to help further God's work in my life.

God has redirected my steps in most of those cases, but those individuals missed their opportunity to be part of it. I have gone around mountains more times than necessary because the people God was going to use to get me beyond those peaks chose to serve themselves over furthering the Mission.

Let me give you a metaphor that I hope will energize you to get on Mission in this relational area.

> *The king's heart is in the hand of the LORD,*
> *Like the rivers of water;*
> *He turns it wherever He wishes.*
> Proverbs 21:1 NKJV

What is a river? Naturally, we think a river is a body of water, but that's not completely true. A river is a hollowed out channel of earth that water flows through. What purifies river water? The water is purified through minerals that are released from the broken rocks and stones in the riverbed. In the same manner, our lives are "purified" through brokenness and the humble submission we give to God as we allow His Spirit to fill our "soul canisters." Jesus stated that:

> "And whosoever shall fall on this stone <u>shall be broken</u>: but on whomsoever it shall fall, it will grind him to powder."
> Matthew 21:44 KJV (emphasis mine)

As we embrace our brokenness for the sake of Christ and the Spirit's Mission, the river of God's Spirit flows through us, directing our courses. But rivers don't remain autonomous. They connect to *other* tributaries. In other words, as we are broken before God in humble submission and we live according to the Mission, He brings other rivers, or similar people, into our lives. What happens in nature when one tributary connects with another?

Power, force, torrent.

As God connects us together with other like-minded, Spirit-motivated individuals, we collectively become even more powerful. We create stronger bonds in the Spiritual realm. The choice is ours. We can choose to remain in our own stream, eventually filled with brackish water and disconnected from the desires that God has for us to further His will in the lives of others; or we can partner with the God of the

ON MISSION: RELATIONSHIP MOMENTUM

Universe, striving for greater connection points and connecting others to other streams, and watch as power, force, and vitality come to all that have been connected.

I will leave you with a final verse. Please let the words set in as you glean your own significance.

> *"There is a river <u>whose streams</u> make glad the city of God,"*
> Psalm 46:4 NASB (emphasis mine)

That is a scripture on Mission.

CHAPTER 27:

ACTIVATING KINGDOM ACTION

As we learn to humbly sanctify ourselves, as our will and His will begin to fuse, we become more than just Spirit listeners; we become Kingdom activators.

Like the site surveyor story, the Holy Spirit does not accomplish His Mission on His own. He requires "vessels" to assist Him in the process.

Therefore, if anyone cleanses himself from these things, he will be <u>a vessel</u> for honor, <u>sanctified</u>, useful to the Master, prepared for every good work.

II Tim. 2:21, NASB (emphasis mine)

Your *entire life* can become activated for the Kingdom, but first you must recognize your divine calling as an image bearer.

Each one of us has a specific purpose, a divine calling that we may or may not realize at this immediate moment. For the next few pages, I'd like to give you some guiding principles that will help you activate the Kingdom in your current position and help you move into your divine placement.

Wherever you are, work with excellence:
Do you know the difference between "destiny" and "destination?" In church circles, we tend to see our "destiny" as a future event, vocation, or opportunity that we have yet to achieve, but that is really your "destination." "Destiny" is the character, skillsets and zeal inside you at this moment. Hopefully, those around you recognize that destiny and, in that recognition, they promote and elevate you into your next destination.

Take for example, the story of Joseph in Genesis. As a young man, God knew of Joseph's future destination: the palace in Egypt as Pharaoh's top official. At the time, Joseph did not have the internal "destiny" to handle the task, so God worked circumstances in Joseph's life in order for Joseph's destiny to match up with Joseph's destination.

Perhaps the best picture of this relationship between destiny and destination can be found in the Dreamworks' animated film, *Joseph, King of Dreams*. As Joseph lies in a prison in Egypt for a crime he did not commit, his heart grows cold and angry. He has just interpreted the dreams of the baker and cupbearer, and they have been released, leaving him wallowing in a dark, rat infested cell. Joseph lashes out at God while attempting to climb the wet cell walls, but he slips on the rocks and comes crashing down onto the hard cell floor. In the center of the cell floor is a tiny, sickly bush the cupbearer had attempted to nurture during his prison time.

As Joseph looks at the nearly dead shrub, he notices a single green leaf hanging off the last seemingly dead branch. Joseph gets up and props up the lifeless bush with a large stick. The movie then goes into a montage, as movies always do, with Joseph reflecting over his life while he waters the tree, nurturing it back to health. In the background, we hear a song entitled *"You Know Better than I."* Here are the last lines of the song:

For, You know better than I
You know the way
I've let go the need to know why
I'll take what answers you supply
You know better than I

As the song ends, we see Joseph adding water to a fresh, vital tree in the middle of a dark prison cell. The moment Joseph removes the stick that had supported the tree during its rehabilitation process, his prison cell door opens and Joseph is released.

God is constantly attempting to water our lives with purpose and character. As we focus on increasing our internal destiny, he's already preparing our next destination. As our internal destiny matches our external destination, God removes the stick. If you want to grasp how God views the limitlessness of your potential, consider the following verse:

> *"If you have raced with men on foot and they have worn you out, how can you compete with horses?"*
> Jeremiah 12:5 NIV

In God, the limitlessness of your potential is tempered with the expanse of your circle of influence. Joseph needed nearly two decades of destiny building because his destination made him responsible for millions of lives. God isn't focused on individual success, but the impact on the sphere of influence that the success brings. This answers a question that Solomon was plagued with: Why to the righteous appear to stagnate and yet the wicked prosper? It is because the enemy of mankind doesn't care who gets destroyed when you move into a destination you don't have the destiny to support. To the enemy, it's not about the destination, it's about the lives you will negatively affect, disillusion, or destroy when your lack of destiny causes you to implode.

Whatever you do, surround yourself with wise counsel:
Our internal destiny is not something we can *personally* use as a currency. Destiny has to be recognized by others. Therefore, you need to surround yourself with those that are wise and discerning enough to

ascertain your internal destiny and influential enough to help promote you to your next destination.

We tend to develop relationships based on how they make us feel, not based on their wisdom, discernment and character. We seek out people that we enjoy going to the ball game or grabbing a beer or coffee with, but we rarely look for those that can peer into our lives and offer us sage advice and further our destinations. This is not to say that we can't have friends we can just "hang" with, but if that is our entire relationship pool, we can often geld ourselves of the opportunities God has for us.

It's important to recognize that personality never trumps character. In other words, you may have a lot of friends that enjoy your company, but may never want to see you accelerate beyond your current destination due to their own jealousy, bitterness, and the like. Ask yourself these questions: If I were to thrust into a place of prominence and accolade tomorrow, would my friends be jealous? Would they attempt to capitalize on my successes? Or would they be the first to congratulate me, and help push me even further?

This question can also be asked of those in authority over you in your current vocation. Are those individuals in leadership focused on your success, or are they working to stagnate your future? Joseph's brothers saw the destiny in their brother, and so they threw him in a pit and sold him into slavery. Do everything you can in your life to distance yourselves from those with that type of "brother" mentality, in both your personal and professional life.

156 MISSION

Wherever you are currently, figure out where God has designed you to operate.

We have each been designed by God with traits, skillsets, and personality and leadership profiles meticulously crafted for specific plans and opportunities. We often fail to realize God's calling on our lives because we get caught in the vocational minutia of our current location.

To figure out specifically what God has called you to, ask yourself this question. "If I were the CEO of my company, what is the *first thing* I would change?" For some, it might be the way that the employees are treated. Chances are you are designed by God to work with people in a human resource or customer service capacity. Maybe the first thing you would do would be to retrofit the finances of the operation. Chances are you would best be suited to be in the accounting field. Perhaps you might create a new product for the company. Chances are you are designed to be an inventor or product developer. Notice that your mind went to a specific area *immediately*. Begin to ask God to help to cultivate that feeling and help orchestrate the steps necessary to propel you toward that particular "destination."

Wherever you end up, make sure Christ and His Spirit are Chairman of the Board

This requires more than putting a fish on a business card, or hanging up a cross on the office wall. Both are great ideas, but having Christ and the Holy Spirit as Chairman of the Board is recognizing that every aspect of your business or work environment can further the Kingdom Mission. If you own a software company, daily go to God and ask, "How can Your Spirit infuse our creativity and programming today?" Remember, the Mission is more than just dialog; it's allowing the Spirit to accomplish His agenda through every outlet at our disposal. Here's the amazing part, often we'll have no idea how that outcome will look.

I have a dear friend named Dave who started an energy bar company. Even that last sentence description is grossly incomplete because he is really *changing the face of nutrition,* using an energy bar company as his mechanism. Now, he didn't come from the nutrition field. He had little background in food preparation or chemistry. He simply believed that he heard the Spirit of God one day tell him, *"Start an energy bar company."*

Since he didn't know anything about the field or its dynamics, he followed the plan outlined in this chapter. He worked with excellence and consulted wise advisors, bringing together the best of the best in their respective fields. He also listened to the voice of the Spirit, and the Spirit was specific. Remember, this wasn't his background and certainly not his expertise. Therefore, if he felt the Spirit say, "Add this ingredient," he did it. If the Spirit said, "Mix the ingredients in this manner," he did it.

You might say, "Well, that's a little far-fetched. He may be placing a little too much trust in that still, small voice." So let's look at the results. Currently, he has scientists and flavor experts around the world marveling at his accomplishments in ingredient combination and taste. He has championship athletes adding his bars to their dietary programs.

He has individuals take one bite of the product and ask to partner with his company.

And he has no idea where it's going to lead.

Sure he has plans, but every day he inquires of the Holy Spirit, "what would you have me to do *today*?" Who knows? He may soon create a product that changes the tide of malnutrition around the world. He may develop a bar, and already is working on it, that staves off some of the world's most prevalent diseases.

Bottom line, with Christ and His Spirit as his Chairman of the Board, the possibilities are endless, and unknown. Only God knows *the end from the beginning*, but Dave *is* living that verse in Jeremiah:

"If you have raced with men on foot and they have worn you out, how can you compete with horses?"
Jeremiah 12:5 NIV

Dave, through the power and counsel of the Spirit, is running with horses. Dave is a man on Mission.

CHAPTER 28:

THE FINAL FORMULA

As we venture toward the close of this journey, I'd like to provide you with a framework of understanding that I hope will carry you well beyond the pages of this book. This insight is something that not only can be adopted by individuals, but also by entire church congregations. It comes in the way of a formula.

One thing that differentiates Christianity from other religious systems is that Christianity is not very formulaic. Though there are a few universal promises, we know that salvation is not contingent on following a set of rules to the letter. Jesus didn't make it easy on us either, healing one man's blindness by touching his eyes and another by mixing his own saliva with mud. I'm sure you have often heard, and I can thankfully profess, Christianity is not a religion, it is a relationship.

I do believe that looking through scripture, we can extract a formula for the Mission. It is a formula that not only penetrates deeply at the individual level, but also becomes a mandate for the ecclesia, the whole body of Christ. I do believe that it is a simple formula that can be understood, adopted and executed with relative ease and extreme passion. So here it is.

GOD'S IMAGE...

BECOMING GOD'S CHILDREN...

FILLED WITH GOD'S ESSENCE...

TO ACCOMPLISH GOD'S MISSION

It's almost too simple, until you break it down:

"GOD'S IMAGE..."

God clearly stated that ALL people are made in the image of God. Sadly, certain churches or individuals often attempt to deny that reality. Those individuals that don't look like those in the church; act according to what they feel are God's holy standards; or practice lifestyles or belief systems that go against God's will, are often, through their dialog and actions, stripped of their "image of God heritage.". We have all seen the media spotlight those waving banners of animosity at the funerals of those practicing same-sex lifestyles, but it can also be heard through the DELIVERY of real truth laced with anger, hatred and disdain, as you learned in the *(Self) "Righteous" Anger* chapter. To see anyone made in the image of God with hatred or enmity is to view those people through satanic lenses. It is the enemy that hates mankind, and when we strip people of their image of God heritage we partner with that agenda. We must first and foremost recognize that everyone is made in the image of God.

"BECOMING GOD'S CHILDREN…"

The Mission is propagated through the lives of those that accept Christ, turn from their sins, and begin emulate Christ both in action and nature. Therefore, Evangelism is a central component of the Mission. As born-again believers, we long for people to experience salvation, to enter into this new life. We must recognize, however, that salvation is the beginning of the journey, not the end. As we share the love of Christ with others, and encourage them to join in the Mission, we see the Kingdom of God manifest in greater measure. We must still remember, however, that we can't do it alone.

"FILLED WITH GOD'S ESSENCE…"

As you have read, you have been given a helper, the Holy Spirit. It is the Holy Spirit's Mission that we partner with, not simply the other way around. Here is where we must be discerning. And as we learned from the *Resistance* section, in the lives of some persons, the Spirit often becomes a phenomenological experience. The born-again believer's walk frequently becomes based on how the Spirit makes them "feel" and they often venture from conference to conference, event to event, searching for the next phenomenological experience.

"TO ACCOMPLISH GOD'S MISSION"

The purpose of the Spirit is not just for the phenomenological experience, although those moments are part of the benefit of His wonder. Instead, it is to partner with Him to complete His unfinished agenda, what I have been calling in this book: the Mission. Remember the verse from chapter 4? "SIT AT MY RIGHT HAND, UNTIL I MAKE ALL YOUR ENEMIES A FOOTSTOOL FOR YOUR FEET" – which was spoken by God, to Christ, but we learned were the Spirit's marching orders? It is the Spirit's assignment. After we start becoming like Christ, in Spirit/will synergy, it becomes *our Mission*.

The Spirit most often accomplishes God's agenda through Jesus' joint heirs. This is the taking up our role as stewards in Christ's prayer of *"Thy Kingdom Come, thy will be done, on Earth as it (already) is in heaven."* (parenthesis mine) Second to praising God, *"Hollowed be thy name"*, it was the next declaration of Christ in his example of how we should pray and what we should pray for. You can pretty much repeat, "Hollowed be thy name, thy Kingdom Come..." without taking a breath. The church must recognize our Mission mandate and help mankind and the earth once again reach God's "in the garden" desire for all of His creation and regain His desired intimacy with mankind, in the here and now.

THE HOLISTIC POWER OF THE FORMULA

Notice that in every stage, GOD is the focus. Churches or individuals that focus on themselves, centered on their own ministry agendas and programs, may miss out on the Mission. They are simply too busy fulfilling their own desires to engage in the Mission of the Kingdom.

WHAT MUST WE DO?

First, we must recognize that all persons are made in the image of God. We must begin with empathy and compassion, not just because people are lost and caught up in sin, but also because that sin is destroying them holistically. We need to understand how sin operates, and why God would have exacted certain mandates. We need to speak beyond the moralism of the world's actions and instead address and expose the debilitating outcomes.

Then we must recognize the role of the Spirit in God's Kingdom agenda. Throughout this book, I have attempted to both unveil the role of the Spirit, and to strip away at the "kooky" persona that the enemy of mankind has attempted to label Him with. We cannot build the Kingdom without Him. It is like being on a construction site with a hammer, nails, and wood and being told to build a five-story castle without a blueprint, a foreman, or previous carpentry experience. Chances are you could build *something*, but it's doubtful you could complete the requested task.

In the same manner, I believe that you have probably been doing much of what has been spoken about in this book. You have been doing it because you love God and also because the Spirit of God, among other things, leads you to repentance and transformation. I have simply shown you how to be more intentional.

One of the most common things people tell me after I give a talk is that I am able to create a framework of language around what they have believed or attempted to practice for years. We can pick up a basketball for the first time and possibly make a basket, but once we are given the rules and framework of the game, an entire world unfolds to us. We can push boundaries; we can train with purpose.

That is my hope for you as you finish this book. I hope that it has encouraged and inspired you; but more than that, I hope you carry on these words to those around you, to your small group or to those in your church.

I'll leave you with a verse that we've already covered. I only want to say that I believe that you, as a man or woman on Mission, are one of these streams.

"*There is a river whose streams make glad <u>the city of God</u>,*"
Psalm 46:4 NASB (emphasis mine)

Oh, and let's add just one more verse…

"And I John saw <u>the holy city</u>, new Jerusalem, coming down from God out of heaven, prepared as a bride adorned for her husband."
Revelation 21:2 KJV (emphasis mine)

Live inspired.

ACKNOWLEDGEMENTS

Over the course of my writing history, I worked on a particular book for over nine years. This book came together in less than a month. Due to the speed and clarity of this book, I have to acknowledge that this writing went far beyond my ken, and that the Spirit of God was the great orchestrator in this venture. I must also recognize those individuals that had a hand in this book.

First, I would like to thank my wife and children for the support. They have always been encouraging, understanding the tension of juggling a business and pursuing my passions.

I would like to thank Dr. Brian Miller, a trusted friend and theological juggernaut, who has helped shape my nuanced and empathetic viewpoint of the world. I would like to thank my men's group from Fairfax Community Church, and the technology that Skype affords to allow me to be part of the group from 800 miles away.

I would like to thank Valerie Cathell for all her encouraging comments through both books. I would especially like to thank Karen Costanzo for her selfless offering of editing this book. I would like to thank Dave Dalton of Ebars for the early morning sessions hashing out the various concepts presented in this book.

Finally, I would like to thank Scott MacLeod of Provision International and his Thunder School students and interns for the opportunity to speak on this topic, and to turn my notes into the structure of this book.

This book was a pleasure and revelation to write. I hope it encourages and inspires you to take the Mission beyond the pages of this book. Feel free to connect with me at david@purefusionmedia.com.